Everything Your Heirs Need To Know

Your Assets, Family History and Final Wishes

David S. Magee

❖❖❖❖❖❖

Dearborn
Financial Publishing, Inc.

To Dorothy
and our heirs
with love

While a great deal of care has been taken to provide accurate and current information, the ideas, suggestions, general principles and conclusions presented in this book are subject to local, state and federal laws and regulations, court cases and any revisions of same. The reader is thus urged to consult legal counsel regarding any points of law—this publication should not be used as a substitute for competent legal advice.

Publisher: Kathleen A. Welton
Associate Editor: Karen A. Christensen
Project Editor: Linda S. Miller
Cover and Interior Design: Lucy A. Jenkins

© 1991 by David S. Magee

Published by Dearborn Financial Publishing, Inc.

Printed in the United States of America

91 92 93 10 9 8 7 6 5 4 3 2

ISBN: 0-79310-126-3

Contents

CHAPTER 9   Final Wishes and Guide for Survivors

Burial and entombment • Cremation • Bequeathal to a medical school • Donation of body parts • Uniform Anatomical Gift Act • Funeral services • Memorial services • Memorial societies

CHAPTER 10   Miscellaneous Information

DOCUMENT POCKETS

Pockets are provided at the back of the book as a place to store photocopies of papers and documents of value to your heirs.

Pocket #1.   Birth certificates • Death certificates • Marriage certificates • Change of name certificates • Divorce decrees or judgments • Annulment decrees or judgments • Adoption papers • Naturalization papers • Other

Pocket #2.   Educational certificates • Educational transcripts • Organization membership certificates • Organization awards • Civic awards • Newspaper articles • Athletic awards • Dramatic awards • Other

Pocket #3.   Life insurance policies • Medical and health insurance policies • Residence insurance policies • Vehicle insurance policies • Other

Pocket #4.   Social Security card • Medicare card • Military separation papers • Military awards • Pension agreements • IRA agreements • 401(k) agreements • Keogh plan agreements • Worker's Compensation award • Railroad retirement documents • Other

Pocket #5.   Savings account books • Safe-deposit box key • Credit union account books • Other

Pocket #6.   Stockbroker account number • Deeds, leases, mortgages • Automobile certificates of title • Stockbroker statements • Judgments • Decrees • Other

Pocket #7.   Copy of will • Power of attorney • Copy of living trust agreement • Other

Pocket #8.   Funeral prearrangement agreement • Funeral prepayment agreement • Cemetery deed • Mausoleum deed • Body bequeathal papers • Uniform donor card • Other

Acknowledgments

My entire family has continually encouraged this project and has assisted in the preparation of this book. I gratefully thank my wife, Dorothy, for all of her help and assistance in discussing, planning and typing the manuscript. My son and my daughters and their husbands have given excellent suggestions, which I have used. My thanks to them—Sandy and Tom Burr, Pat and Rick Yuille, Judy and Richard Dugan and Dave Magee, Jr. (A special thanks to Judy, whose first-published book ignited the spark for this one.) Herbert A. Milliken, Jr., Howard L. Gay and John W. Olson were kind enough to take their valuable time to read the manuscript and constructively criticize it. My thanks to Maryann Murphy for allowing the use of her graphics studio in the book's production. Thanks also to Sally Jaeger, Shelly Lowenkopf, Jody Joseph and many good friends who have offered valuable suggestions and support. Finally, for time spent far and beyond the call of friendship, I thank Richard L. Rapport, M.D., for his enthusiastic encouragement and for the many hours he spent editing the manuscript.

Introduction

It is easy to estimate that several billion dollars now held in stocks, bonds, insurance, bank accounts and other assets around the country will never be claimed by the rightful owners. New York state alone already has an unclaimed property fund that tops a billion dollars.

The bulk of this fortune lies unclaimed because heirs to these assets have no idea their inheritances exist. It is not lack of concern for heirs or for the destiny of personal assets that creates this growing untapped treasure. Certainly most of us would much prefer to see the fruits of our lifelong efforts benefit loved ones rather than landing in state coffers.

Why then are so many heirs unaware of property intended for them? The answer is simply that many people fail to leave their families a clear record of their assets. The widespread habit of filing important papers in shoe boxes, bottom drawers and scattered files leaves families searching months, even years, for needed papers and records—and the search will not even begin if the family does not know an asset exists.

One California family was recently tracked down by private investigators for a company that had sold stock to their father over 20 years before. Since no record of the $500 in stock was found after the father's death, the family was not aware of his investment. Thanks to the company's president, who had personally sold the stock to their father and hired the investigators, the heirs were located just one week before the state was to claim the assets. The $500 in stock? It is now worth $160,000. This family was fortunate; most heirs to unrecorded assets never know their inheritances exist.

Comedian W.C. Fields was an extreme case. Memories of his impoverished youth brought Fields recurring nightmares about being stranded in a strange city without funds. The wealthy performer recalled opening as many as 700 bank accounts, often in fictitious names, in the cities he visited around the world. Fields left no record for his heirs and only 48 of his bank accounts were located after his death. Over a million dollars of his estate is thought to have remained scattered in hundreds of undiscovered bank accounts.

While few of us have 700 bank accounts (much less the million to put in them), we may have picked up a couple of life insurance policies, bought a few shares of stock or opened an extra savings account or two over the years. We also can probably locate the papers to prove it, perhaps with a little digging. The question is whether anyone else can.

A will that fully outlines assets is all that is needed then, right? Not true. In the first place, few people update their wills with each acquisition or sale of personal property. Also, wills often simply divide estates into bulk portions, mentioning major assets and leaving heirs, executors and the courts to determine the remaining contents of the estate. Without clear records, the family is faced with the burdensome and often costly task of locating records, papers and documents to establish the extent of the estate.

Certain major assets are not even typically included in wills. Life insurance proceeds, pensions, Social Security and veteran benefits all have fixed plans of distribution unaffected by wills, and so they are not commonly mentioned. A clear, up-to-date listing of available assets and benefits can prove invaluable to your heirs. This book is designed to make that easy to provide.

Also of value to the family is a record of personal wishes regarding funeral and burial arrangements. Many people live together for 50 years without discussing their wishes. Without intent, they leave many distressing decisions for their loved ones. You can spare your family this distress by simply deciding upon and recording your own preferences. A will, however, is not the best place for detailing final arrangements, since wills are often read after the burial. This book discusses various arrangements that can be made and provides a place to express your wishes.

Perhaps the most cherished legacy you can provide your heirs is your unique knowledge of family history, your recollections about your own life, interests and accomplishments, and other special remembrances. These can be shared in the first section of the book.

At the end of the book, you will find pockets to store papers and documents so they will be readily available to your heirs. By gathering these papers and the facts suggested on the pages that follow, you will be able to organize your affairs and provide an invaluable guide for your heirs.

A GUIDE TO THIS BOOK

The first part of each chapter contains information for you and your heirs. This is followed by forms designed for you to provide your heirs with a detailed personal record of your assets, family history, final wishes and other notes for your heirs.

The document pockets at the end of the book provide a place for storing birth certificates, marriage certificates, funeral prearrangement agreements and other papers that will be of value to your heirs. Any original documents that are irreplaceable or have intrinsic value (stock certificates, bonds, etc.) should be kept in a safe-deposit box, with copies in the document pockets.

There is no need to complete the forms in the order in which they appear. It may be more enjoyable to go through a first time jotting down information that is readily available. Then you may go back and fill in the missing pieces.

You may find that some forms do not apply to you. If so, indicate that they do not apply and go on. *If the forms do apply to you, fill them in.* Even though you may not have all of the answers at first, take the time to find them. You know the sources; your heirs may not.

Fill in the forms with a soft lead pencil. If your decisions change as time goes by, it will be easy to erase what you have previously written and insert new directions for your heirs. Or, if you prefer ink, correct with typewriter correction fluid.

Print legibly. After all, if you take the time to organize this record for your heirs, you want them to be able to read it.

Keep the forms up-to-date. As changes occur, update the forms. It is a good plan to review them at least once a year.

Discuss this book with your heirs. They must be aware of its existence, know where it is located and know what it says in order for it to be of value to them. Although for many people death is a difficult subject to discuss, this feeling should be overcome. Sit down and have a frank and open talk with those closest to you.

It is unlikely that you will be able to complete this guide in one or two sittings. Some information will take extra thought or research. But don't look upon it as a task. If you approach it in manageable sections and look upon it as a fascinating family project, you will find it can give you great satisfaction to track down bits and pieces of your family history, locate the missing birth certificate and gradually put your affairs in order. These records can be of great interest and value to you during your lifetime. But the greatest satisfaction will be in knowing that should anything happen to you, your loved ones will have your notes, your wishes and the information that you have provided to guide them.

❖❖❖❖❖❖

TO YOUR HEIRS:

A "Guide for Survivors" can be found in Chapter 9. This provides a list of steps to be taken at a time of family loss with references to appropriate pages in this book.

CHAPTER 1

Personal History

No one knows your personal history as well as you do. Do your children know where you were born? Where you went to school? In what cities you have lived? Your mother's family name? Where your parents lived or are buried? The different types of work experiences you have had? The hobbies and clubs you have enjoyed through the years? Probably not.

And yet, haven't you asked yourself many of these questions in regard to your own parents? Or your grandparents? Or your brothers and sisters? Most of us become more interested in family history as we age. If someone does not record the facts, they will be lost. *You* are the one who can do this best.

Go through the forms in Chapter 1 and fill in the answers that you know. There will be many blanks when you finish. Make gathering the rest of the answers an enjoyable project. Telephone or drop a note to a parent, brother, sister, aunt, uncle, son or daughter and gradually complete your personal history. As a bonus, you may rekindle family ties.

GENERAL OUTLINE

The forms in Chapter 1 are set out in the following order:
General summary
Marital background
Children
Parents
Grandparents
Brothers and sisters
My educational background
My work background
My religion, politics and hobbies

My organizations, unions, clubs, etc.

My residences

Miscellaneous

The form entitled "General Summary" provides a place for you to record pertinent facts of your life.

Forms are provided for three spouses, six children and five siblings. If needed, you may photocopy extra forms and keep them in Document Pocket #1. Excess forms may be removed from the book, keeping in mind that families change in unforseen ways as a result of births, deaths, divorces and marriages.

Many of the forms have space provided on the back where you may write personal notes about your relatives. You may choose to give a brief history, to discuss their beliefs or accomplishments, or to share personal reminiscences. Use the space as you wish.

The remaining forms in Chapter 1 seek more detailed information about you—your educational background, where you have worked and lived, organizations you have joined, your religion, politics and hobbies. Photocopies of related certificates, articles, and awards can be kept in Document Pocket #2.

Finally, you will find a form entitled "Miscellaneous." This is for *you* to fill in with personal notes about yourself or your family—your interests, accomplishments, thoughts or desires. Add anything you consider to be of interest to your family and heirs. Don't be modest! If you did something in your lifetime of which you are proud, tell them about it. They will be proud, too. If something very humorous happened to you, your heirs will enjoy it. Remember how you were fascinated with the interesting stories told to you by your mother, father and grandparents? Your heirs are just as interested in your remembrances.

A primary purpose of the forms in Chapter 1 is to provide enjoyment for your heirs. However, there are other purposes. At the time of death, some of this information will be used in the preparation of a death certificate, newspaper obituary, federal estate tax return, state inheritance tax return, income tax return and many other administrative forms.

BIRTH AND MARRIAGE CERTIFICATES

The vast majority of births, deaths and marriages are reported to the proper authorities so that a lasting record can be maintained. There are a number of reasons, however, why it may be difficult to obtain records when they are needed. In the not too distant past, many births occurred in private homes and went unreported. Occasionally, courthouses or other record depositories were destroyed by fire. Records escaping this fate may be incorrect because of typographical errors, misunderstanding of names and other errors that are bound to occur.

There may be a long delay after a request for copies of certificates while records are corrected or reestablished. It is a good idea to request them now so they will always be on hand.

It is suggested that you have in your possession two *certified* copies each of your birth certificate, your spouse's birth certificate, your marriage certificate and the birth certificates of your dependent children.

Each state has its own method of maintaining these records. They can usually be obtained from the county clerk, registrar or recorder of the county in which the birth or marriage took place. Many states have a central clearing house for this at the state capital, generally called the Department of Vital Statistics.

There is no standard fee for providing these records. Fees generally range from $2 to $20. Additional copies may be available at reduced rates.

To expedite the sometimes lengthy procedure of obtaining records, first inquire about the price for copies of specific certificates. Include a self-addressed, stamped envelope with your price request. Once you know the price, you can write for the copies you need, enclosing the necessary payment. Use a money order or bank check, rather than your personal check, for prompt service.

Many states will not issue copies of birth or marriage certificates unless the requestor is closely related to the person named in the certificate. It is important to identify yourself as spouse, mother or father.

You can store these certificates in Document Pocket #1.

DECREES AND JUDGMENTS OF DIVORCE AND ANNULMENT

It may be necessary for you to have certified copies of judgments of divorce or annulment for Social Security benefits, veteran benefits and private pension plans. These may be obtained from the clerk or registrar of the court that granted the divorce or annulment. Once again, the fee for obtaining copies will vary among the states and may depend upon the number of pages in the document.

Write a letter to the court that granted the decree or judgment to inquire about the cost of obtaining a copy of the document. Note the date and year the divorce or annulment was granted and be sure to enclose a self-addressed, stamped envelope.

GENERAL SUMMARY

My Personal History

My full name at present: _____
                                 First   *Middle*   *Last*

My full name at birth: _____
                            First   *Middle*   *Last*

Place of birth: _____
                City   *County*   *State*   *Country*

Date of birth: _____ Social Security #: _____

A certified copy of my birth and/or adoption certificate is located: _____

_____

My legal name was changed to: _____
                                 First   *Middle*   *Last*

on _____ by _____
    Date   *Name of court*

located at _____
                  City   *State*

A certificate of my legal name change is located: _____

_____

Year residence established in this state: _____ this community: _____

My usual occupation: _____ Industry: _____

I am a citizen of: _____ ☐ by birth or ☐ by naturalization.

I was naturalized on: _____ at _____
                    Date   *Place*

Naturalization #: _____

My naturalization papers are located: _____

Military veteran: ☐ Yes ☐ No Branch of service: _____

Dates of service: _____ Serial #: _____ Final rank: _____

Marital status: ☐ Never married ☐ Married ☐ Divorced ☐ Widowed

My present address: _____
                    Street address and apartment number

_____ _____ _____ _____
Telephone #   *City*   *State*   *ZIP code*

GENERAL SUMMARY

My Personal History

Marriages
Sp = Spouse

	Full Name of Spouse at Birth	Last Name at Present or at Death	Date of Birth	Death
Sp #1				
Sp #2				
Sp #3				

(See pages 7–13 for further information about my spouses.)

Children
Ch = Child

	Full Name of Child at Birth	Last Name at Present or at Death	Date of Birth	Death
Ch #1				
Ch #2				
Ch #3				
Ch #4				
Ch #5				
Ch #6				

(See pages 15–38 for further information about my children.)

Brothers and Sisters (Siblings)
Si = Sibling

	Full Name of Brother or Sister at Birth	Last Name at Present or at Death	Date of Birth	Death
Si #1				
Si #2				
Si #3				
Si #4				
Si #5				

(See pages 49–58 for further information about my brothers and sisters.)

MARITAL BACKGROUND

My Personal History

☐ I have never been married.

☐ I have been married _____ time(s) during my life.

Sp = Spouse

	Name of Spouse (Before Marriage)	Date of Marriage	Place of Marriage
Sp #1			
Sp #2			
Sp #3			

	Number of Children	Date Marriage Ended by Death	Divorce	Place Marriage Ended
Sp #1				
Sp #2				
Sp #3				

I have in my possession certified copies of the following documents:

	Marriage Certificate Yes	No	Divorce Decree Yes	No	Death Certificate Yes	No
Sp #1						
Sp #2						
Sp #3						

The above legal documents are located:

_____

_____

_____

_____

_____

_____

MARITAL BACKGROUND

My First Spouse

Full name at present: _____
                      First   *Middle*   *Last*

Full name at birth: _____
               First   *Middle*   *Last*

Place of birth: _____
          City   *County*   *State*   *Country*

Date of birth: _____   Social Security #: _____

Citizen of _____   ☐ by birth or ☐ by naturalization

Date of marriage: _____   Place of marriage: _____

Present address: _____
          Street address and apartment number

_____ _____
Telephone #   *City*   *State*   *ZIP code*

Date of death: _____   Cause of death: _____

He/she was buried at: _____ Lot #: _____
          Name of cemetery

_____
City   *State*

Or: He/she was cremated and the ashes were: _____

Or: He/she donated his/her body to: _____
                        Name of medical school

We were divorced on: _____   at: _____
          Date   *City*   *State*

We had the following children:

	Date of Birth	Full Name at Birth	Present Last Name
#1			
#2			
#3			
#4			
#5			
#6			

MARITAL BACKGROUND

My First Spouse

_____

_____

_____

_____

_____

_____

_____

_____

_____

_____

_____

_____

_____

_____

_____

_____

_____

_____

_____

_____

_____

_____

_____

_____

MARITAL BACKGROUND

My Second Spouse

Full name at present: _____
    First   Middle   Last

Full name at birth: _____
    First   Middle   Last

Place of birth: _____
    City   County   State   Country

Date of birth: _____ Social Security #: _____

Citizen of _____ ☐ by birth or ☐ by naturalization

Date of marriage: _____ Place of marriage: _____

Present address: _____
    Street address and apartment number

_____ _____
Telephone #   City   State   ZIP code

Date of death: _____ Cause of death: _____

He/she was buried at: _____ Lot #: _____
    Name of cemetery

_____
    City   State

Or: He/she was cremated and the ashes were: _____

Or: He/she donated his/her body to: _____
    Name of medical school

We were divorced on: _____ at: _____
    Date   City   State

We had the following children:

	Date of Birth	Full Name at Birth	Present Last Name
#1			
#2			
#3			
#4			
#5			
#6			

MARITAL BACKGROUND

My Second Spouse

_____

_____

_____

_____

_____

_____

_____

_____

_____

_____

_____

_____

_____

_____

_____

_____

_____

_____

_____

_____

_____

_____

_____

_____

_____

MARITAL BACKGROUND

My Third Spouse

Full name at present: _____
                           First   *Middle*   *Last*

Full name at birth: _____
           First   *Middle*   *Last*

Place of birth: _____
    City   *County*   *State*   *Country*

Date of birth: _____ Social Security #: _____

Citizen of _____ ☐ by birth or ☐ by naturalization

Date of marriage: _____ Place of marriage: _____

Present address: _____
    Street address and apartment number

_____
Telephone #   *City*   *State*   *ZIP code*

Date of death: _____ Cause of death: _____

He/she was buried at: _____ Lot #: _____
    Name of cemetery

_____
City   *State*

Or: He/she was cremated and the ashes were: _____

Or: He/she donated his/her body to: _____
    Name of medical school

We were divorced on: _____ at: _____
    Date   *City*   *State*

We had the following children:

	Date of Birth	Full Name at Birth	Present Last Name
#1			
#2			
#3			
#4			
#5			
#6			

MARITAL BACKGROUND

My Third Spouse

CHILDREN

My First Child

Child's full name at present: _____
                              First   *Middle*   *Last*

Child's full name at birth: _____
                            First   *Middle*   *Last*

Date of birth: _____ Place of birth: _____
                                             City   *County*   *State*   *Country*

Adopted? _____ (If so, give details on reverse.) Social Security #: _____

Citizen of: _____ ☐ by birth or ☐ by naturalization

Present address: _____
                 Street address and apartment number

_____   _____
Telephone #   *City*   *State*   *ZIP code*

Date of death: _____ Cause of death: _____

Child is buried at: _____ Lot #: _____
                    Name of cemetery

_____
City   *State*

Or: Child was cremated and the ashes were: _____

Or: Child donated body to: _____
                             Name of medical school

☐ Child has never married.

☐ Child has been married _____ times. The names of the child's spouses, marriage dates, etc., are as follows:

	Name of Spouse (Before Marriage)	Date of Birth	Date of Marriage	Date of Death	Divorce
#1					
#2					
#3					

CHILDREN

My First Child

CHILDREN

My First Child's Children

Child's full name at present: _____

☐ Never had any children.

☐ Had _____ children.

Gch = Grandchild

	Full Name of My Grandchild at Birth	Last Name at Present or at Death	Date of Birth	Date of Death
Gch #1				
Gch #2				
Gch #3				
Gch #4				
Gch #5				
Gch #6				

	Name of Grandchild's Present Spouse	Address
Gch #1		
Gch #2		
Gch #3		
Gch #4		
Gch #5		
Gch #6		

CHILDREN

My First Child's Children

_____

_____

_____

_____

_____

_____

_____

_____

_____

_____

_____

_____

_____

_____

_____

_____

_____

_____

_____

_____

_____

_____

_____

CHILDREN

My Second Child

Child's full name at present: _____
First   Middle   Last

Child's full name at birth: _____
First   Middle   Last

Date of birth: _____ Place of birth: _____
City   County   State   Country

Adopted? _____ (If so, give details on reverse.) Social Security #: _____

Citizen of: _____ ☐ by birth or ☐ by naturalization

Present address: _____
Street address and apartment number

_____ _____
Telephone # *City*   *State*   *ZIP code*

Date of death: _____ Cause of death: _____

Child is buried at: _____ Lot #: _____
Name of cemetery

_____
City   *State*

Or: Child was cremated and the ashes were: _____

Or: Child donated body to: _____
Name of medical school

☐ Child has never married.

☐ Child has been married _____ times. The names of the child's spouses, marriage dates, etc., are as follows:

	Name of Spouse (Before Marriage)	Date of Birth	Date of Marriage	Date of Death	Divorce
#1					
#2					
#3					

CHILDREN

My Second Child

CHILDREN
My Second Child's Children

Child's full name at present: _____

☐ Never had any children.

☐ Had _____ children.

Gch = Grandchild

	Full Name of My Grandchild at Birth	Last Name at Present or at Death	Date of Birth	Death
Gch #1				
Gch #2				
Gch #3				
Gch #4				
Gch #5				
Gch #6				

	Name of Grandchild's Present Spouse	Address
Gch #1		
Gch #2		
Gch #3		
Gch #4		
Gch #5		
Gch #6		

CHILDREN

My Second Child's Children

CHILDREN

My Third Child

Child's full name at present: _____
First   Middle   Last

Child's full name at birth: _____
First   Middle   Last

Date of birth: _____ Place of birth: _____
City   County   State   Country

Adopted? _____ (If so, give details on reverse.) Social Security #: _____

Citizen of: _____ ☐ by birth or ☐ by naturalization

Present address: _____
Street address and apartment number

_____ _____ _____ _____
Telephone #   City   State   ZIP code

Date of death: _____ Cause of death: _____

Child is buried at: _____ Lot #: _____
Name of cemetery

_____ _____
City   State

Or: Child was cremated and the ashes were: _____

Or: Child donated body to: _____
Name of medical school

☐ Child has never married.

☐ Child has been married _____ times. The names of the child's spouses, marriage dates, etc., are as follows:

	Name of Spouse (Before Marriage)	Date of Birth	Date of Marriage	Date of Death	Divorce
#1					
#2					
#3					

CHILDREN
My Third Child

CHILDREN

My Third Child's Children

Child's full name at present: _____

☐ Never had any children.

☐ Had _____ children.

Gch = Grandchild

	Full Name of My Grandchild at Birth	Last Name at Present or at Death	Date of Birth	Date of Death
Gch #1				
Gch #2				
Gch #3				
Gch #4				
Gch #5				
Gch #6				

	Name of Grandchild's Present Spouse	Address
Gch #1		
Gch #2		
Gch #3		
Gch #4		
Gch #5		
Gch #6		

CHILDREN

My Third Child's Children

CHILDREN

My Fourth Child

Child's full name at present: _____
                                       First   *Middle*   *Last*

Child's full name at birth: _____
                                  First   *Middle*   *Last*

Date of birth: _____ Place of birth: _____
                                               City   *County*   *State*   *Country*

Adopted? _____ (If so, give details on reverse.) Social Security #: _____

Citizen of: _____ ☐ by birth or ☐ by naturalization

Present address: _____
                                 Street address and apartment number

_____ _____
Telephone #   *City*   *State*   *ZIP code*

Date of death: _____ Cause of death: _____

Child is buried at: _____ Lot #: _____
                    Name of cemetery

_____
     City   *State*

Or: Child was cremated and the ashes were: _____

Or: Child donated body to: _____
                                 Name of medical school

☐ Child has never married.

☐ Child has been married _____ times. The names of the child's spouses, marriage dates, etc., are as follows:

	Name of Spouse (Before Marriage)	Date of Birth	Date of Marriage	Date of Death	Divorce
#1					
#2					
#3					

CHILDREN

My Fourth Child

CHILDREN

My Fourth Child's Children

Child's full name at present: _____

☐ Never had any children.

☐ Had _____ children.

Gch = Grandchild

	Full Name of My Grandchild at Birth	Last Name at Present or at Death	Date of Birth	Death
Gch #1				
Gch #2				
Gch #3				
Gch #4				
Gch #5				
Gch #6				

	Name of Grandchild's Present Spouse	Address
Gch #1		
Gch #2		
Gch #3		
Gch #4		
Gch #5		
Gch #6		

CHILDREN

My Fourth Child's Children

CHILDREN

My Fifth Child

Child's full name at present: _____
$\qquad\qquad\qquad\qquad$ *First* $\qquad\qquad$ *Middle* $\qquad\qquad$ *Last*

Child's full name at birth: _____
$\qquad\qquad\qquad\qquad$ *First* $\qquad\qquad$ *Middle* $\qquad\qquad$ *Last*

Date of birth: _____ Place of birth: _____
$\qquad\qquad\qquad\qquad\qquad\qquad$ *City* $\qquad$ *County* $\qquad$ *State* $\qquad$ *Country*

Adopted? _____ (If so, give details on reverse.) Social Security #: _____

Citizen of: _____ ☐ by birth or ☐ by naturalization

Present address: _____
$\qquad\qquad\qquad$ *Street address and apartment number*

_____ _____
Telephone # $\quad$ *City* $\qquad\qquad\qquad\qquad\qquad$ *State* $\qquad\qquad$ *ZIP code*

Date of death: _____ Cause of death: _____

Child is buried at: _____ Lot #: _____
$\qquad\qquad\qquad$ *Name of cemetery*

_____
$\qquad$ *City* $\qquad\qquad\qquad\qquad\qquad$ *State*

Or: Child was cremated and the ashes were: _____

Or: Child donated body to: _____
$\qquad\qquad\qquad\qquad\qquad$ *Name of medical school*

☐ Child has never married.

☐ Child has been married _____ times. The names of the child's spouses, marriage dates, etc., are as follows:

	Name of Spouse (Before Marriage)	Date of Birth	Date of Marriage	Date of Death	Divorce
#1					
#2					
#3					

CHILDREN

My Fifth Child

CHILDREN

My Fifth Child's Children

Child's full name at present: _____

☐ Never had any children.

☐ Had _____ children.

Gch = Grandchild

	Full Name of My Grandchild at Birth	Last Name at Present or at Death	Date of Birth	Death
Gch #1				
Gch #2				
Gch #3				
Gch #4				
Gch #5				
Gch #6				

	Name of Grandchild's Present Spouse	Address
Gch #1		
Gch #2		
Gch #3		
Gch #4		
Gch #5		
Gch #6		

CHILDREN

My Fifth Child's Children

CHILDREN

My Sixth Child

Child's full name at present: _____
                                            First   *Middle*   *Last*

Child's full name at birth: _____
                                    First   *Middle*   *Last*

Date of birth: _____ Place of birth: _____
                                                City   *County*   *State*   *Country*

Adopted? _____ (If so, give details on reverse.) Social Security #: _____

Citizen of: _____ ☐ by birth or ☐ by naturalization

Present address: _____
                    Street address and apartment number

_____ _____
Telephone #   *City*   *State*   *ZIP code*

Date of death: _____ Cause of death: _____

Child is buried at: _____ Lot #: _____
                  Name of cemetery

_____
     City   *State*

Or: Child was cremated and the ashes were: _____

Or: Child donated body to: _____
                                 Name of medical school

☐ Child has never married.

☐ Child has been married _____ times. The names of the child's spouses, marriage dates, etc., are as follows:

	Name of Spouse (Before Marriage)	Date of Birth	Date of Marriage	Date of Death	Divorce
#1					
#2					
#3					

CHILDREN

My Sixth Child

CHILDREN

My Sixth Child's Children

Child's full name at present: _____

☐ Never had any children.

☐ Had _____ children.

Gch = Grandchild

	Full Name of My Grandchild at Birth	Last Name at Present or at Death	Date of Birth	Date of Death
Gch #1				
Gch #2				
Gch #3				
Gch #4				
Gch #5				
Gch #6				

	Name of Grandchild's Present Spouse	Address
Gch #1		
Gch #2		
Gch #3		
Gch #4		
Gch #5		
Gch #6		

CHILDREN

My Sixth Child's Children

PARENTS

Father

Full name at present: _____
        First   *Middle*   *Last*

Full name at birth: _____
        First   *Middle*   *Last*

Place of birth: _____
     City   *County*   *State*   *Country*

Date of birth: _____

Present address: _____
      Street address and apartment number

_____ _____
Telephone # *City*   *State*   *ZIP code*

Date of death: _____ Cause of death: _____

Buried at: _____ Lot #: _____
   Name of cemetery

_____
City   *State*

Or: Cremated and ashes were: _____

_____

Or: Donated body to: _____
        Name of medical school

My parents were married on: _____ at: _____

_____
      City   *State*

My parents were divorced on: _____ at: _____
          Date   *City*   *State*

☐ Never married.

☐ Married _____ times.

	Name of Spouse (Before Marriage)	Date of Marriage	Date of Death	Date of Divorce
#1				
#2				
#3				

PARENTS

Father

PARENTS

Mother

Full name at present: _____
First   Middle   Last

Full name at birth: _____
First   Middle   Last

Place of birth: _____
City   County   State   Country

Date of birth: _____

Present address: _____
Street address and apartment number

_____
Telephone #   City   State   ZIP code

Date of death: _____ Cause of death: _____

Buried at: _____ Lot #: _____
Name of cemetery

_____
City   State

Or: Cremated and ashes were: _____

_____

Or: Donated body to: _____
Name of medical school

My parents were married on: _____ at: _____

_____
City   State

My parents were divorced on: _____ at: _____
Date   City   State

☐ Never married.

☐ Married _____ times.

	Name of Spouse (Before Marriage)	Date of Marriage	Date of Death	Divorce
#1				
#2				
#3				

PARENTS

Mother

_____

_____

_____

_____

_____

_____

_____

_____

_____

_____

_____

_____

_____

_____

_____

_____

_____

_____

_____

_____

_____

_____

_____

_____

_____

GRANDPARENTS

My Father's Parents

GRANDFATHER

My grandfather's full name at birth: _____
First   Middle   Last

Place of birth: _____
City   County   State   Country

Citizen of: _____   ☐ by birth or ☐ by naturalization

Date of birth: _____   Date of death: _____

My grandfather is buried at: _____ Lot #: _____
Name of cemetery

_____
City   State

Or: My grandfather was cremated and his ashes were: _____

Or: My grandfather donated his body to: _____
Name of medical school

☐ My grandfather married _____ times.

☐ My grandfather never married.

	Name of Wife (Before Marriage)	Date of Marriage	Date of Death	Date of Divorce
#1				
#2				
#3				

❖❖❖❖❖❖

GRANDMOTHER

My grandmother's full name at birth: _____
First   Middle   Last

Place of birth: _____
City   County   State   Country

Citizen of: _____   ☐ by birth or ☐ by naturalization

Date of birth: _____   Date of death: _____

GRANDPARENTS

My Father's Parents

My grandmother is buried at: _____ Lot #: _____

Name of cemetery

_____

City   *State*

Or: My grandmother was cremated and her ashes were: _____

Or: My grandmother donated her body to: _____

Name of medical school

☐ My grandmother married _____ times.

☐ My grandmother never married.

	Name of Husband	Date of Marriage	Date of Death	Date of Divorce
#1				
#2				
#3				

❖❖❖❖❖❖

My grandparents were married on: _____ at: _____

_____

City   *State*

My grandparents were divorced on: _____ at:_____

Date   *City*   *State*

☐ My grandparents never married.

GRANDPARENTS

My Father's Parents

_____

_____

_____

_____

_____

_____

_____

_____

_____

_____

_____

_____

_____

_____

_____

_____

_____

_____

_____

_____

_____

_____

GRANDPARENTS

My Mother's Parents

GRANDFATHER

My grandfather's full name at birth: _____
                                         First   *Middle*   *Last*

Place of birth: _____
                 City   *County*   *State*   *Country*

Citizen of: _____ ☐ by birth or ☐ by naturalization

Date of birth: _____ Date of death: _____

My grandfather is buried at: _____ Lot #: _____
                            Name of cemetery

_____
        City   *State*

Or: My grandfather was cremated and his ashes were: _____

Or: My grandfather donated his body to: _____
                            Name of medical school

☐ My grandfather married _____ times.

☐ My grandfather never married.

	Name of Wife (Before Marriage)	Date of Marriage	Date of Death	Date of Divorce
#1				
#2				
#3				

✦✦✦✦✦✦

GRANDMOTHER

My grandmother's full name at birth: _____
                                 First   *Middle*   *Last*

Place of birth: _____
                 City   *County*   *State*   *Country*

Citizen of: _____ ☐ by birth or ☐ by naturalization

Date of birth: _____ Date of death: _____

GRANDPARENTS

My Mother's Parents

My grandmother is buried at: _____ Lot #: _____
Name of cemetery

_____
City   *State*

Or: My grandmother was cremated and her ashes were: _____

Or: My grandmother donated her body to: _____
Name of medical school

☐ My grandmother married _____ times.

☐ My grandmother never married.

	Name of Husband	Date of Marriage	Date of Death	Date of Divorce
#1				
#2				
#3				

❖❖❖❖❖❖

My grandparents were married on: _____ at: _____

_____
City   *State*

My grandparents were divorced on: _____ at:_____
Date   *City*   *State*

☐ My grandparents never married.

GRANDPARENTS

My Mother's Parents

BROTHERS AND SISTERS

My First Sibling

Full name at present: _____
                                   First   *Middle*   *Last*

Full name at birth: _____
                              First   *Middle*   *Last*

Place of birth: _____
              City   *County*   *State*   *Country*

Citizen of: _____ ☐ by birth or ☐ by naturalization

Date of birth: _____ Date of death: _____

This sibling is related to me by: ☐ full blood   ☐ half blood   ☐ adoption
                                   (common parents)   (one common parent)

If related by half blood, or adopted, sibling's parents (or adopting parents) were:

Mother: _____ Father: _____

Sibling's present address: _____
                             Street address and apartment number

_____
Telephone #   *City*   *State*   *ZIP code*

Sibling is buried at: _____ Lot #: _____
                   Name of cemetery

_____
        City   *State*

☐ Sibling has never married. ☐ Sibling has been married _____ times.

	Name of Spouse (Before Marriage)	Date of Marriage	Date of Death	Date of Divorce
#1				
#2				
#3				

☐ Sibling has had _____ children born alive, or adopted; or ☐ sibling has never had any children.

	Full Name of Child at Birth (My Nieces and Nephews)	Last Name at Present or at Death	Date of Birth	Date of Death
#1				
#2				
#3				
#4				
#5				
#6				

BROTHERS AND SISTERS

My First Sibling

_____

_____

_____

_____

_____

_____

_____

_____

_____

_____

_____

_____

_____

_____

_____

_____

_____

_____

_____

_____

_____

_____

_____

_____

_____

BROTHERS AND SISTERS

My Second Sibling

Full name at present: _____
　　　　　　　　　　　　　　　　First　　　　　　　　*Middle*　　　　　　　　*Last*

Full name at birth: _____
　　　　　　　　　　　　　　　First　　　　　　　　*Middle*　　　　　　　　*Last*

Place of birth: _____
　　　　　　　　　　　　City　　　　　　*County*　　　　　*State*　　　　*Country*

Citizen of: _____　☐ by birth　or　☐ by naturalization

Date of birth: _____　Date of death: _____

This sibling is related to me by:　☐ full blood　　☐ half blood　　　☐ adoption
　　　　　　　　　　　　　　　　　　　(common parents)　(one common parent)

If related by half blood, or adopted, sibling's parents (or adopting parents) were:

　Mother: _____　Father: _____

Sibling's present address: _____
　　　　　　　　　　　　　　Street address and apartment number

_____　_____
Telephone #　　　　*City*　　　　　　　　　　*State*　　　　*ZIP code*

Sibling is buried at: _____　Lot #: _____
　　　　　　　　　　Name of cemetery

_____
　　City　　　　　　　　　　　　　　　　　*State*

☐ Sibling has never married.　☐ Sibling has been married _____ times.

	Name of Spouse (Before Marriage)	Date of Marriage	Date of Death	Divorce
#1				
#2				
#3				

☐ Sibling has had _____ children born alive, or adopted; or ☐ sibling has never had any children.

	Full Name of Child at Birth (My Nieces and Nephews)	Last Name at Present or at Death	Date of Birth	Death
#1				
#2				
#3				
#4				
#5				
#6				

BROTHERS AND SISTERS
My Second Sibling

BROTHERS AND SISTERS

My Third Sibling

Full name at present: _____
                            First   *Middle*   *Last*

Full name at birth: _____
                            First   *Middle*   *Last*

Place of birth: _____
                    City   *County*   *State*   *Country*

Citizen of: _____ ☐ by birth or ☐ by naturalization

Date of birth: _____ Date of death: _____

This sibling is related to me by: ☐ full blood   ☐ half blood   ☐ adoption
                                     (common parents)   (one common parent)

If related by half blood, or adopted, sibling's parents (or adopting parents) were:

  Mother: _____ Father: _____

Sibling's present address: _____
                              Street address and apartment number

_____ _____ _____ _____
Telephone #   *City*   *State*   *ZIP code*

Sibling is buried at: _____ Lot #: _____
                        Name of cemetery

_____ _____
City   *State*

☐ Sibling has never married. ☐ Sibling has been married _____ times.

	Name of Spouse (Before Marriage)	Date of Marriage	Date of	
			Death	Divorce
#1				
#2				
#3				

☐ Sibling has had _____ children born alive, or adopted; or ☐ sibling has never had any children.

	Full Name of Child at Birth (My Nieces and Nephews)	Last Name at Present or at Death	Date of	
			Birth	Death
#1				
#2				
#3				
#4				
#5				
#6				

BROTHERS AND SISTERS

My Third Sibling

_____

_____

_____

_____

_____

_____

_____

_____

_____

_____

_____

_____

_____

_____

_____

_____

_____

_____

_____

_____

_____

_____

_____

_____

_____

BROTHERS AND SISTERS

My Fourth Sibling

Full name at present: _____
                              First   Middle   Last

Full name at birth: _____
                              First   Middle   Last

Place of birth: _____
                        City   County   State   Country

Citizen of: _____ ☐ by birth or ☐ by naturalization

Date of birth: _____ Date of death: _____

This sibling is related to me by: ☐ full blood   ☐ half blood   ☐ adoption
                                          (common parents)   (one common parent)

If related by half blood, or adopted, sibling's parents (or adopting parents) were:

  Mother: _____ Father: _____

Sibling's present address: _____
                                  Street address and apartment number

_____   _____
Telephone #   City   State   ZIP code

Sibling is buried at: _____ Lot #: _____
                        Name of cemetery

_____
City   State

☐ Sibling has never married.   ☐ Sibling has been married _____ times.

	Name of Spouse (Before Marriage)	Date of Marriage	Date of Death	Divorce
#1				
#2				
#3				

☐ Sibling has had _____ children born alive, or adopted; or ☐ sibling has never had any children.

	Full Name of Child at Birth (My Nieces and Nephews)	Last Name at Present or at Death	Date of Birth	Death
#1				
#2				
#3				
#4				
#5				
#6				

BROTHERS AND SISTERS

My Fourth Sibling

BROTHERS AND SISTERS

My Fifth Sibling

Full name at present: _____
First   Middle   Last

Full name at birth: _____
First   Middle   Last

Place of birth: _____
City   County   State   Country

Citizen of: _____ ☐ by birth or ☐ by naturalization

Date of birth: _____ Date of death: _____

This sibling is related to me by: ☐ full blood   ☐ half blood   ☐ adoption
                                 (common parents)   (one common parent)

If related by half blood, or adopted, sibling's parents (or adopting parents) were:

Mother: _____ Father: _____

Sibling's present address: _____
Street address and apartment number

_____ _____ _____ _____
Telephone #   City   State   ZIP code

Sibling is buried at: _____ Lot #: _____
Name of cemetery

_____ _____
City   State

☐ Sibling has never married. ☐ Sibling has been married _____ times.

	Name of Spouse (Before Marriage)	Date of Marriage	Date of Death	Divorce
#1				
#2				
#3				

☐ Sibling has had _____ children born alive, or adopted; or ☐ sibling has never had any children.

	Full Name of Child at Birth (My Nieces and Nephews)	Last Name at Present or at Death	Date of Birth	Death
#1				
#2				
#3				
#4				
#5				
#6				

BROTHERS AND SISTERS
My Fifth Sibling

MY EDUCATIONAL BACKGROUND

Personal History

I attended the following elementary schools:

Name of School	Location	Grades Attended	Dates Attended

I attended the following junior high schools (or middle schools):

Name of School	Location	Grades Attended	Dates Attended

I attended the following high schools (or preparatory schools):

Name of School	Location	Grades Attended	Dates Attended	Graduated?

I attended the following institutions of higher learning:

Name of Institution	Location	Degree	Dates Attended

MY EDUCATIONAL BACKGROUND

Personal History

I was involved in the following extracurricular activities: (List athletics, debating, drama, music, art, school newspaper, etc.)

_____

_____

_____

_____

_____

_____

_____

_____

_____

_____

I received the following educational honors, scholarships, commendations, etc.: (List details.)

_____

_____

_____

_____

_____

_____

_____

_____

_____

MY WORK BACKGROUND

Personal History

Names of Primary Employers	Location	Dates	Type of Work

☐ I retired from work on: _____ .
Date

☐ I am presently employed (describe name and address of employer or place of self-employment, type of work, etc.):

_____

_____

_____

_____

Describe any interesting facts, over the years, concerning employment:

_____

_____

_____

_____

MY WORK BACKGROUND

Personal History

MY RELIGION, POLITICS AND HOBBIES

Personal History

My religious memberships, activities and beliefs are as follows:

_____

_____

_____

_____

_____

_____

My political memberships, activities and beliefs are as follows:

_____

_____

_____

_____

_____

_____

Over the years, my hobbies have been:

_____

_____

_____

_____

_____

_____

MY RELIGION, POLITICS AND HOBBIES

Personal History

_____

_____

_____

_____

_____

_____

_____

_____

_____

_____

_____

_____

_____

_____

_____

_____

_____

_____

_____

_____

_____

_____

_____

_____

_____

MY ORGANIZATIONS, UNIONS AND CLUBS

Personal History

I have belonged to the following organizations, unions, clubs, etc. (List all such organizations, with dates of membership, offices held, etc. If the organization is not commonly known, describe it.)

_____

_____

_____

_____

_____

_____

_____

_____

_____

_____

_____

_____

_____

_____

_____

_____

_____

_____

_____

_____

_____

MY RESIDENCES

Personal History

I lived in the following towns, cities and states at the street addresses listed:

Address	City	State	Dates

MISCELLANEOUS

Personal History

The following miscellaneous notes regarding my personal history may be of interest to my heirs:

_____

_____

_____

_____

_____

_____

_____

_____

_____

_____

_____

_____

_____

_____

_____

_____

_____

_____

_____

_____

_____

_____

_____

_____

_____

MISCELLANEOUS

Personal History

CHAPTER 2

Insurance

Insurance offers a way to spread the risk of financial loss among many people. The payment of an annual premium protects the insured (to the limits of the policy) against losses from fire, theft, accident, liability, etc. Any loss is shared by all of those insured, saving the individual from financial disaster. The group, in other words, absorbs the individual's unexpected losses.

Life insurance is primarily intended to ease the financial loss to a beneficiary that results from the policyholder's death. Although death comes to everyone and cannot be considered "unexpected" in the long run, it can certainly be unexpected when it occurs. If something should happen to you—death, an accident, a stroke or other circumstance that prevents you from acting on your own behalf—your loved ones may have to file claims, cancel certain policies or obtain new ones in order to protect your property. Many policies go unclaimed because the family or heirs were never told about them. For these reasons, it is important that your loved ones know about all of your insurance policies. The forms in this chapter are provided to list your various policies with the names and addresses of the agents and companies.

The following is not a detailed breakdown of the many types of insurance available. It should, however, give you some information about the most widely used coverages in order to help you organize your own policies. You may wish to photocopy your policies and keep them in Document Pocket #3.

LIFE INSURANCE

A life insurance policy pays a designated sum of money to the beneficiary upon the death of the insured. This money may be paid in a lump sum, in a monthly sum for the life of another, in monthly sums over a certain period of time, or in some other manner spelled out by the terms of the policy. Regardless of the method of payment, the sum is designated in the provisions of the policy. It may even pay double if your death is caused by accident—a so-called "double indemnity" policy.

A widely purchased form of life insurance is *whole life insurance.* This type of coverage provides a sum of money (face value) to be paid to the beneficiary at the time of the insured's death. The insured has paid the same annual premium since taking out the policy. The amount of the premium is determined by the age of the individual at the time the policy was purchased. The younger the purchaser, the smaller the premium on the policy. Variations in the method of payment for whole life insurance are available. For example, you might obtain a policy which requires annual premiums for 20 years. At the expiration of the 20-year period, the policy continues in effect for the balance of your life, but no more premiums are required. It is even possible to purchase a policy by making one large initial premium payment. Regardless of the method of payment, whole life insurance provides coverage for the rest of your life.

Universal life is a form of permanent life insurance in which the policyholder may vary the premium from year to year. The cash value reserve in the policy is credited with an interest-rated base on short-term investments and is adjusted periodically. A full disclosure is made to the policyholder each year, showing the interest credited, expense charges and the pure cost of the insurance protection.

Variable whole life and *variable universal life* are forms of permanent insurance in which the cash value reserves are invested in equity investments, i.e., stocks and bonds. The policyholder is able to select the investment from the menu offered by the insurance company.

When purchasing any "permanent" type of life insurance policy, be careful not to pay premiums into the policy in excess of the amount allowed under the Internal Revenue Code. If you exceed the limit in any of the first seven years, your policy will be treated as a "modified endowment contract" for tax purposes and any money subsequently borrowed or withdrawn from the policy will be taxed as interest rather than investment withdrawal or premiums paid. This applies to policies purchased after June 21, 1988.

Term insurance, on the other hand, provides insurance coverage only for a specified length of time. That is, you might purchase a policy which provides coverage for 5 years, 10 years or 20 years. The annual premium for term insurance is substantially less than the annual premium for whole life insurance. For example, a typical annual premium for a one-year term policy might be $2 to $3 per $1,000 at age 25. The cost of purchasing the same coverage would gradually increase with the age of the purchaser. By age 55, that same coverage could run between $10 and $15 per $1,000, or about five times the price given a 25-year-old. On the other hand, whole life insurance might start around $10 per $1,000 at age

25. The premiums would remain at that level throughout the life of the insured. To take out the same coverage at age 55, however, might run from $30 to $45 per $1,000, or three to four times the price given a 25-year-old.

Many term life insurance contracts provide that the policy may be renewed at the end of the term without providing further proof of insurability. The premium for the renewed term will be higher than for the original term. Other term policies provide that they may be converted, within a certain period of time, into a permanent type of life or endowment insurance without proof of insurability. Once again, the premium would be adjusted.

Regardless of the type of life insurance you hold, it is important that the insurance policies be readily available at death, that the heirs know their location and that they be kept in a safe place. The policy must be surrendered to the insuring company at the time of payment of the proceeds. Although there is a procedure which may be followed in the case of a lost policy, there may be a long delay in collecting the proceeds from the company.

Many employers provide life insurance for employees. Partnerships often fund buy-sell agreements with life insurance. Be sure to include information about work-related insurance in the forms.

MEDICAL, HEALTH, DISABILITY, ACCIDENT AND TRAVEL INSURANCE

Health insurance provides a means for paying hospital and medical expenses arising from sickness and accident. In addition, disability insurance policies are available to provide money for loss of income when an individual is unable to work because of sickness or accidental injury.

Many different types of accident and illness insurance policies exist. Some are so limited in scope that it seems necessary to be gored by a bull while riding a streetcar between midnight and 3:00 A.M. in order to collect on the policy. Other policies, however, provide very broad coverage, though each has its limitations.

Travel policies were the forerunners of the present-day health and accident policies. Travel policies may limit coverage to airplanes, automobiles, boats and motorcycles, or they may cover an insured individual during a specified policy period, like the length of a vacation or business trip.

Medical expense reimbursement policies range from a policy that pays $10 for each day the insured is hospitalized to policies that cover almost every health expense that the policyholder could incur. Because the coverages vary to such a great extent, the cost of health and accident coverage varies.

During the last three or four decades, Blue Cross–Blue Shield plans have been widely used throughout the country. A relatively new idea in health care insurance that is gaining popularity is offered through health maintenance organization plans (HMOs). This form of health insurance enables a person to contract with a group of physicians who have joined together to provide specific health services for a designated annual fee. The HMO group may offer its services in a certain hospital or clinic, or the physicians within the group may be scattered in offices and hospitals throughout the community. (The latter is known as an Independent Practice Association, or IPA.) In addition, *major medical coverage* is available to pick up expenses not covered by a basic health and accident policy.

VEHICLE INSURANCE

Automobile insurance should be considered a necessity by the owner of any motor vehicle. In fact, many states require all drivers to be insured for liability to other persons for damages resulting from an automobile accident. Regardless of the law, it only makes good sense to insure yourself against the claims of others and against a loss that you might sustain as the result of collision, fire or theft of your automobile.

Liability coverage protects you, to the extent of the coverage that you have purchased, against the claims of persons who claim to have been injured or damaged as a result of the operation of your motor vehicle. The policy not only provides for payment of the claim, but also pays legal and other expenses for the defense of any claim.

Collision coverage pays for damage sustained by your automobile in a collision or upset. It is usually subject to a deductible amount that you must pay if you are at fault.

Comprehensive coverage, along with fire, theft and windstorm coverage, protects the insured from damage (other than damage caused by accident) to his or her own automobile.

Similar coverages are available for motorcycles, motorboats, snowmobiles and other vehicles.

Uninsured motorists' insurance protects the persons in the insured vehicle when involved in an accident with an uninsured motorist. The insurance, for all practical purposes, provides liability coverage for the uninsured motorist; and the injured persons can look to their own insurance company to cover their losses—rather than to an uncollectible individual.

Underinsured motorists' insurance protects the person in the insured vehicle involved in an accident with a motorist who is underinsured. If, for example, the person in the insured vehicle sustained $50,000 of personal injuries because of the negligence of a motorist who only has $20,000 of liability coverage, the underinsured motorists' insurance would pay the excess over $20,000 up to the coverage limits purchased by the insured.

No-fault liability for motor vehicle accidents has been adopted by many states. Although provisions of the different laws vary, the general idea of no-fault liability is that automobile owners must provide their own insurance for any injuries or property damage sustained, regardless of who was to blame for the accident.

Except in certain circumstances (as established by states' no-fault laws), an "injured person" cannot sue the other driver to recover any damages. In those states that have adopted the no-fault concept, the law requires that motorists maintain no-fault insurance on their vehicles. Generally, if you do not carry no-fault insurance, you are not only violating the law, but you have no place to seek repayment of your losses, even if you are not at fault in an accident.

TO YOUR HEIRS

At time of death, the vehicle insurance company should be notified so there will be complete coverage during the period before the vehicle's assignment to its next owner.

RESIDENCE INSURANCE

Originally, fire insurance was about the only type of insurance that a home owner could obtain on his or her residence. As the various insurance lines developed, insurance became available to protect against windstorm, hail, explosion, riot, smoke damage, etc. Insurance also became available for the contents of the home, as well as for outbuildings.

Today, most homeowners purchase a "homeowners' policy," which combines fire and extended coverage insurance on the dwelling with protection for personal property, additional living expense, comprehensive personal liability coverage, medical payments and physical damage to property of others. Rather than being required to search out individual policies covering all of these various risks, the homeowners' policy combines them.

Similar types of policies are available to the condominium owner and apartment dweller. The policy can be tailor-made to fit specific needs by the addition of standard forms.

Upon your death, your heirs should immediately contact your insurance agent to ensure that your home and contents are properly insured during the administration of your estate.

ADDITIONAL LIABILITY PROTECTION

Many insurance companies offer additional liability protection through an *umbrella policy*, which provides insurance coverage in excess of your regular automobile, personal liability and other liability coverages. It is usually sold in multiples of $1 million, and is a low-cost method of buying substantial protection.

INSURANCE POLICIES

Life Insurance

*Types of insurance policies: WH = Whole Life UN = Universal Life TM = Term
DI = Double Indemnity VUL = Variable Universal Life VWL = Variable Whole Life O = Other*

(The above abbreviations may be used to describe the different types of insurance policies you carry.)

☐ I do not carry insurance policies.

☐ I carry the following insurance policies:

Company: _____ Type of policy: _____

Agent (if any): _____

Address of ☐ company or ☐ agent: _____

_____

_____

Policy #: _____ Face amount: _____

Beneficiary(ies): _____

❖❖❖❖❖

Company: _____ Type of policy: _____

Agent (if any): _____

Address of ☐ company or ☐ agent: _____

_____

_____

Policy #: _____ Face amount: _____

Beneficiary(ies): _____

❖❖❖❖❖

Company: _____ Type of policy: _____

Agent (if any): _____

Address of ☐ company or ☐ agent: _____

_____

_____

Policy #: _____ Face amount: _____

Beneficiary(ies): _____

INSURANCE POLICIES

Life Insurance

Types of insurance policies: WH = Whole Life   UN = Universal Life   TM = Term
DI = Double Indemnity   VUL = Variable Universal Life   VWL = Variable Whole Life   O = Other

(The above abbreviations may be used to describe the different types of insurance policies you carry.)

☐ I do not carry insurance policies.

☐ I carry the following insurance policies:

Company: _____ Type of policy: _____

Agent (if any): _____

Address of ☐ company or ☐ agent: _____

_____

_____

Policy #: _____ Face amount: _____

Beneficiary(ies): _____

❖❖❖❖❖❖

Company: _____ Type of policy: _____

Agent (if any): _____

Address of ☐ company or ☐ agent: _____

_____

_____

Policy #: _____ Face amount: _____

Beneficiary(ies): _____

❖❖❖❖❖❖

Company: _____ Type of policy: _____

Agent (if any): _____

Address of ☐ company or ☐ agent: _____

_____

_____

Policy #: _____ Face amount: _____

Beneficiary(ies): _____

INSURANCE POLICIES

Life Insurance

*Types of insurance policies: WH = Whole Life   UN = Universal Life   TM = Term
DI = Double Indemnity   VUL = Variable Universal Life   VWL = Variable Whole Life   O = Other*

(The above abbreviations may be used to describe the different types of insurance policies you carry.)

☐ I do not carry insurance policies.

☐ I carry the following insurance policies:

Company: _____ Type of policy: _____

Agent (if any): _____

Address of ☐ company or ☐ agent: _____

_____

_____

Policy #: _____ Face amount: _____

Beneficiary(ies): _____

❖❖❖❖❖❖

Company: _____ Type of policy: _____

Agent (if any): _____

Address of ☐ company or ☐ agent: _____

_____

_____

Policy #: _____ Face amount: _____

Beneficiary(ies): _____

❖❖❖❖❖❖

Company: _____ Type of policy: _____

Agent (if any): _____

Address of ☐ company or ☐ agent: _____

_____

_____

Policy #: _____ Face amount: _____

Beneficiary(ies): _____

INSURANCE POLICIES

Residence Insurance

☐ I do not carry residential insurance.

☐ I carry residential insurance policies with the following companies (list all policies including fire, windstorm, theft, personal liability, homeowners, etc.):

Company: _____

Agent (if any): _____

Address of ☐ company or ☐ agent: _____

_____

_____

Policy #: _____

Description of coverage: _____

_____

❖❖❖❖❖❖

Company: _____

Agent (if any): _____

Address of ☐ company or ☐ agent: _____

_____

_____

Policy #: _____

Description of coverage: _____

_____

❖❖❖❖❖❖

Company: _____

Agent (if any): _____

Address of ☐ company or ☐ agent: _____

_____

_____

Policy #: _____

Description of coverage: _____

_____

INSURANCE POLICIES

Medical, Health, Disability, Accident and Travel

Types of policies:
HO = Hospitalization   *VI = Vision and Eye*   *MD = Medical*
MM = Major Medical   *SU = Surgical*   *ATR = Air Travel*
DI = Disability   *TR = Travel Accidental Death*   *Accidental Death*
DT = Dental   *O = Other*   *MC = Medicare*

(The above abbreviations may be used to describe the different types of insurance policies you carry.)

☐ I carry no medical insurance policies.

☐ I carry the following medical insurance policies:

Company: _____ Type of policy: _____

Agent (if any): _____

Address of ☐ company or ☐ agent: _____

_____

_____

Policy #: _____ Group #: _____ Service code #: _____

❖❖❖❖❖❖

Company: _____ Type of policy: _____

Agent (if any): _____

Address of ☐ company or ☐ agent: _____

_____

_____

Policy #: _____ Group #: _____ Service code #: _____

❖❖❖❖❖❖

Company: _____ Type of policy: _____

Agent (if any): _____

Address of ☐ company or ☐ agent: _____

_____

_____

Policy #: _____ Group #: _____ Service code #: _____

INSURANCE POLICIES

Medical, Health, Disability, Accident and Travel

Types of policies:

HO = Hospitalization	VI = Vision and Eye	MD = Medical
MM = Major Medical	SU = Surgical	ATR = Air Travel
DI = Disability	TR = Travel Accidental Death	Accidental Death
DT = Dental	O = Other	MC = Medicare

(The above abbreviations may be used to describe the different types of insurance policies you carry.)

☐ I carry no medical insurance policies.

☐ I carry the following medical insurance policies:

Company: _____ Type of policy: _____

Agent (if any): _____

Address of ☐ company or ☐ agent: _____

_____

_____

Policy #: _____ Group #: _____ Service code #: _____

❖❖❖❖❖❖

Company: _____ Type of policy: _____

Agent (if any): _____

Address of ☐ company or ☐ agent: _____

_____

_____

Policy #: _____ Group #: _____ Service code #: _____

❖❖❖❖❖❖

Company: _____ Type of policy: _____

Agent (if any): _____

Address of ☐ company or ☐ agent: _____

_____

_____

Policy #: _____ Group #: _____ Service code #: _____

INSURANCE POLICIES

Vehicles: Automobiles, Motorcycles, Boats, Airplanes, etc.

I carry vehicle insurance (including motorcycles, snowmobiles, boats, airplanes, etc.) with the following companies:

Company: _____

Agent (if any): _____

Address of ☐ company or ☐ agent: _____

_____

_____

Policy #: _____

Description of vehicles insured: _____

_____

❖❖❖❖❖❖

Company: _____

Agent (if any): _____

Address of ☐ company or ☐ agent: _____

_____

_____

Policy #: _____

Description of vehicles insured: _____

_____

❖❖❖❖❖❖

Company: _____

Agent (if any): _____

Address of ☐ company or ☐ agent: _____

_____

_____

Policy #: _____

Description of vehicles insured: _____

_____

INSURANCE POLICIES

Vehicles: Automobiles, Motorcycles, Boats, Airplanes, etc.

I carry vehicle insurance (including motorcycles, snowmobiles, boats, airplanes, etc.) with the following companies:

Company: _____

Agent (if any): _____

Address of ☐ company or ☐ agent: _____

_____

_____

Policy #: _____

Description of vehicles insured: _____

_____

✧✧✧✧✧✧

Company: _____

Agent (if any): _____

Address of ☐ company or ☐ agent: _____

_____

_____

Policy #: _____

Description of vehicles insured: _____

_____

✧✧✧✧✧✧

Company: _____

Agent (if any): _____

Address of ☐ company or ☐ agent: _____

_____

_____

Policy #: _____

Description of vehicles insured: _____

_____

CHAPTER 3

Other Benefits

Most of us are aware of retirement benefits from Social Security, certain disability benefits for U.S. military veterans, worker's disability compensation for job-related injuries and illness, and retirement payments from private and public pension plans. But some may be unaware of the benefits from the same sources that may be available to their survivors. This chapter is primarily concerned with benefits that may be available to your survivors. You may wish to photocopy documentation of your various benefits and keep them in Document Pocket #4.

SOCIAL SECURITY

Social Security provides continuing income when family earnings are reduced or stopped because of retirement, disability or death. Nine of ten workers in the United States earn protection under Social Security. The country's aged population has health insurance under Medicare.

Since Social Security legislation was enacted in 1935, many changes have broadened the protection given to workers and their families. Initially, Social Security covered only the worker upon his retirement; but in 1939 the law was extended to pay certain dependents when he retired, as well as paying certain survivors when he died.

Disability insurance benefits were first provided in July 1957, giving workers protection against loss of earnings due to total disability.

The Social Security program was expanded again in 1965 with the enactment of Medicare, which ensured hospital and medical insurance protection to people 65 and over. Since 1973, Medicare coverage has been available to those people under 65 who have been entitled to Social Security disability checks for two or more consecutive years. It also covers people with permanent kidney failure who need dialysis or kidney transplants.

Before you or your family can receive monthly cash benefits, credit must be established for a certain amount of work under Social Security.

The required work credit depends on your age and whether you are applying for retirement, survivor or disability benefits. Information on specific requirements is available at any of the 1,300 Social Security Administration offices located throughout the country.

Retirement checks may be received as early as age 62 and disability checks at any age. Monthly payments can be received by a *retired* or *disabled* worker's

- unmarried children under 18 (or 19 if full-time elementary or high school student);
- unmarried children 18 or over who were severely disabled before age 22, and who continue to be disabled;
- a wife or husband 62 or older who has been married to the worker for at least one year; or
- a wife or husband under 62 if she or he is caring for a child under 16 (or disabled) who is receiving a benefit under the worker's earnings.

A divorced spouse who has been divorced at least two years can receive benefits at 62 regardless of whether his or her former spouse receives them. Their marriage must have lasted ten years or more. The former spouse must be at least 62 and eligible for Social Security benefits, regardless of whether he or she has retired.

Your heirs are primarily affected, however, by benefits that may be available after your death. First, there is a lump-sum payment that can be made where an eligible husband or wife survives or if a child is entitled to survivor benefits.

Social Security survivors insurance can provide cash benefits on the earnings record of a deceased worker to the following:

- A widow or widower—full benefits at 65 or any age if caring for an entitled child (under 16 or disabled) of the deceased worker. Reduced benefits can be received at 60 (or 50 and disabled) if not caring for a child. Remarriage after 60 (50 if disabled) will not prevent the payment of benefits.
- Unmarried children up to 18 (or 19 if they are attending an elementary or secondary school full time). Children who were disabled before 22 can receive benefits at any age as long as they remain disabled.
- Divorced widow or widower if the marriage lasted at least ten years—full benefits at 65 or any age if caring for an entitled child (under 16 or disabled) of the deceased worker. Reduced benefits can be received at 60 (or 50 if disabled). Remarriage after 60 (or 50 if disabled) will not prevent the payment of benefits.
- A mother or father of the worker's child under 16 or disabled, if caring for the child.
- Lump-sum death payment—is a one-time payment of $255. It is paid to the surviving widow(er) who was either living in the same

household as the deceased at the time of death or was eligible for or entitled to survivors benefits on the worker's record for the month of death. If there was no surviving widow(er), it is payable to a child or children eligible for or entitled to survivors benefits on the worker's record for the month the worker died.

In addition, grandchildren, great-grandchildren, and dependent parents 62 or older may qualify for survivors' benefits on the deceased worker's record under certain circumstances.

Medicare, a federal hospital and medical insurance, is available through Social Security to help protect eligible persons 65 and over from the high costs of health care. Also eligible for Medicare are disabled people under 65 who have been entitled to Social Security disability benefits for 24 or more months. Insured workers and their dependents who need dialysis treatment or a kidney transplant because of permanent kidney failure also have Medicare protection at any age.

The *hospital insurance* portion of Medicare helps pay the cost of inpatient hospital care and certain kinds of follow-up care. If you are eligible for Social Security or Railroad Retirement payments, either as a worker, dependent, or survivor, you automatically have *hospital* insurance protection when you are 65.

The *medical insurance* portion of Medicare helps defray costs of physician services, outpatient hospital services, and certain other medical items, as well as services not covered by the hospital insurance. People who have medical insurance pay a monthly premium, but more than two-thirds of the cost of the medical insurance is paid from general revenues of the federal government. Only a small basic premium is charged for the medical insurance. The amount of the premium is adjusted periodically to reflect the cost of the care.

You should apply for your Medicare insurance at least three months before your 65th birthday in order for your protection to start at age 65.

APPLYING FOR SOCIAL SECURITY BENEFITS

When you apply for Social Security benefits, you should have the following with you:
- your own Social Security card or a record of your number (if your claim is on another person's record, you will need that person's card or a record of the number);
- proof of your age (a birth certificate or baptismal certificate made within five years after birth);
- your marriage certificate if you are applying for widower's or widow's benefits;
- your children's birth certificates and Social Security numbers if you are applying for them;

- the deceased worker's W-2 form(s) for the previous year or a copy of his or her last federal income tax return if self-employed. Without this information, those earnings will not be in the Social Security records and cannot be included when benefits are calculated; and
- proof of divorce, if you are applying for benefits as a divorced spouse.

The above information will provide you and your heirs knowledge of certain rights which may be available to you or to them. *Since the Social Security Act can be amended at any time, this may not be the latest available information concerning benefits to which you or your heirs may be entitled. Contact the nearest Social Security Administration for a full explanation of your rights under the law.*

VETERAN BENEFITS

The Veterans Administration is charged with administering benefits available to persons who have served on active duty in the U.S. military service. The benefits depend upon the veteran's length of service, the era during which the service was performed, whether the veteran is disabled, whether the disability was caused by active service, and so many other criteria that it would take another book to set out the specific requirements.

Under certain circumstances, the following benefits (and many more) *may* be available to a veteran:

- pensions for disability caused by service-connected injury or disease
- pensions for certain non-service-connected disabilities
- automobile allowance for service-connected loss, or permanent loss of the use of one or both hands or feet
- hospitalization benefits
- alcohol and drug dependence treatment
- outpatient medical treatment
- prosthetic appliances
- vocational rehabilitation
- loan guaranty benefits
- insurance
- federal civil service preference

Certain benefits are available to your heirs if you were separated from the service under conditions other than dishonorable.

Burial flag. An American flag may be issued to drape the casket of an eligible veteran. After the funeral service, the flag may be given to the next of kin or close friend or associate of the deceased. Flags are issued at any VA office and most local post offices.

Burial in national cemeteries. Any deceased veteran of wartime or peacetime service whose last period of active service terminated other than dishonorably may be buried in a national cemetery. In addition, the spouse, surviving spouse or minor children of an eligible veteran may be buried in a national cemetery. In each instance, space must be available. There is no charge for a grave nor for its opening and closing.

Transportation of deceased veteran to a national cemetery. The VA may pay the cost of transportation of a deceased veteran for burial in a national cemetery if the veteran died of a service-connected disability or the veteran was receiving disability compensation from the VA.

Headstones or markers. The VA will furnish, upon request, a headstone or marker to be placed at the unmarked grave of a veteran whose last discharge was other than dishonorable. This service is provided for eligible veterans whether they are buried in a national cemetery or elsewhere. A headstone or marker is automatically furnished if burial is in a national cemetery. Otherwise, application must be made to the VA. The VA will ship the headstone or marker, without charge, to the person or firm designated on the application. If a nongovernment headstone or marker is used at a veteran's gravesite in other than a national cemetery, a partial reimbursement may be made by the VA. The amount of this payment would not exceed the average actual cost of a government headstone or marker.

Reimbursement of burial expenses. The VA is authorized to pay an allowance toward the funeral and burial expenses of an eligible veteran. A veteran not buried in a national cemetery will be paid an additional allowance for a plot for interment. If the veteran's death is service-connected or if the veteran died in a VA hospital, the VA is authorized to pay a larger sum for the burial and funeral expenses.

Dependency and Indemnity Compensation (DIC). DIC payments are authorized for widows or widowers, children and parents of service personnel who die during active duty as well as veterans whose deaths were service-connected (when death occured on or after January 1, 1957). The exact amount of the basic benefit is determined by the military pay grade of the deceased veteran. Payments are also made for children between 18 and 23 attending school.

Nonservice-connected death pension. Surviving spouses and unmarried children under age 18 (or until age 23 if attending an approved course of study) may be eligible for a pension if their income does not exceed certain limits.

Education for spouses, widows, widowers, sons and daughters. If a veteran is completely disabled or dies as a result of service, the VA will generally (but with some exceptions) pay to help educate the spouse, widow or widower, and each son and daughter beyond the secondary school level.

If you are a veteran, your heirs should seek assistance through the Veterans Administration, or through a local Veteran's Counseling Service, in order to apply for available benefits.

WORKER'S COMPENSATION

Worker's Compensation laws have been adopted by all of the states. Although details vary greatly, the general purpose is to provide income to workers who are unable to work as a result of an injury, or occupational disease, arising out of the worker's employment. While incapacitated, he or she receives a weekly sum based on his or her average wage and number of dependents. In addition, medical expenses related to the injury are paid by the employer or the employer's insurance company.

Here, however, we are primarily interested in Worker's Compensation benefits available to dependents of a deceased employee. Ordinarily, the spouse and minor children of an employee who died as the result of a work-incurred accident, or occupational disease, are entitled to weekly payments for a time. Usually, the spouse is entitled to payments for a specified number of years or until remarriage, whichever is sooner; and the dependent children are entitled to benefits until they reach a certain age.

Usually, the laws also provide that the widowed spouse, or the deceased employee's estate, is entitled to a specific funeral or death benefit.

It is important then, that your heirs be made aware of any life-threatening injuries or occupational diseases incurred during the course of your employment. If your death is subsequently caused by the injury or occupational disease, your dependents may be entitled to substantial monetary benefits.

In the forms provided at the end of this chapter, be sure to detail any of your medical problems that may be related to your employment.

PENSIONS

Many public and private employees are provided pensions through their jobs. Some pensions are entirely financed by the employer, while some are cofinanced by the employer and the employee.

Many persons not covered by a pension through their employment have established individual retirement accounts (IRAs). The law allows a person to contribute a certain sum of tax-deductible income annually to an IRA, which earns money while deferring the payment of income taxes on the contribution and the earnings to a date when it is likely that the person will want to withdraw the assets for use as retirement funds.

There are many other tax-deferred plans, accounts, etc., that can accomplish the same purpose of allowing an individual to defer tax until, theoretically, he or she has reached an age where the most profitable earning years have declined.

Self-employed individuals may establish a Keogh plan or HR 10 plan. These plans allow for larger, tax-deferred yearly contributions and greater benefits than does the IRA.

A simplified employee pension (SEP) allows an employer to make deductible contributions to an employee's IRA.

CODAs give an employee the option to choose to receive cash from the employer or have the employer contribute to a qualified profit-sharing or stock bonus plan on behalf of the employee.

In other words, many types of plans are available—401(k) plans, "savings" plans, segregated asset account plans, annuity plans, etc. From the standpoint of your heirs, it is most vital that they be aware of any plans in which you are a participant. At your death, the particular plan may provide dependency payments to your spouse and/or minor children; may provide a substantial pay-off to a designated beneficiary or to your estate; or may, in fact, provide nothing.

In the forms provided at the end of this chapter, give all of the information to your heirs about any retirement assets in which you have an interest.

OTHER BENEFITS

Social Security

My name (from Social Security card): _____

Social Security #: _____ □ Male or □ Female

I □ have; or □ have never filed an application for monthly Social Security benefits.

If so, said application was filed on □ my earning record or □ the earning record of:

_____
              Full name   *Social Security number*

I received the following kind of monthly benefit: _____
                                              (Retirement, disability, widow, etc.)

I □ have worked; or □ have not worked in the railroad industry at any time after January 1, 1937.*

My military service information is found on my Veteran's Benefits form, page 91.

My marriage history and the facts related to my children are found in the forms located at the end of Chapter 1.

My Medicare information is found in the forms on pages 79–80.

My Social Security card is located: _____

Other documents pertaining to my Social Security status are located: _____

_____

This may affect your Social Security.

OTHER BENEFITS

Veteran Benefits

☐ I have never served in the military service of the United States.

☐ I have served in the military service of the United States.

Full present name: _____
                          First   *Middle*   *Last*

Name served under: _____
                          First   *Middle*   *Last*

V.A. File #: C- _____   Social Security #: _____   Railroad Retirement #: _____

Date of birth: _____   Place of birth: _____

Entered Active Service		Service Number	Separated		Grade or Rank and Branch
Date	Place		Date	Place	

My marriage history and the facts related to my children and my parents are found in the forms at the end of Chapter 1.

My military separation papers are located: _____

_____

I received the following military decorations: _____

_____

The following is a resumé of my military career: _____

_____

_____

_____

_____

(may be continued on reverse)

OTHER BENEFITS

Veteran Benefits

_____

_____

_____

_____

_____

_____

_____

_____

_____

_____

_____

_____

_____

_____

_____

_____

_____

_____

_____

_____

_____

_____

_____

OTHER BENEFITS

Worker's Compensation

☐ I have never received Worker's Compensation benefits.

☐ I have received Worker's Compensation benefits.

Name of employer: _____

Address of employer: _____

_____

_____

Date of injury or occupational disease: _____

Name of insurance company: _____

Address of insurance company: _____

_____

_____

Insurance company's (or self-insured employer's) claim number: _____

Details of injury or occupational disease: _____

_____

_____

Duration of payments: _____

❖❖❖❖❖

In addition to the above, I have received the following serious injuries, or occupational diseases, during the course of my employment:

_____

_____

_____

❖❖❖❖❖

All papers related to my Worker's Compensation claims are located: _____

_____

_____

_____

OTHER BENEFITS

Pensions, etc.

☐ I do not have any pension rights.

☐ I have certain pension rights.

Name of payor: _____

Address of payor: _____

_____

Pension identification number: _____

There ☐ are or ☐ are not benefits under the plan to certain survivors upon my death.

❖❖❖❖❖❖

Name of payor: _____

Address of payor: _____

_____

Pension identification number: _____

There ☐ are or ☐ are not benefits under the plan to certain survivors upon my death.

❖❖❖❖❖❖

I ☐ have or ☐ do not have an individual retirement account (IRA).

Name of institution: _____

Address: _____

_____

IRA account number: _____

❖❖❖❖❖❖

I ☐ have or ☐ do not have a Keogh pension plan.

Name of institution: _____

Address: _____

_____

Keogh account number: _____

OTHER BENEFITS

Pensions, etc.

❖❖❖❖❖❖

I ☐ have or ☐ do not have a 401(k) plan.

Name of institution: _____

Address: _____

_____

401(k) account number: _____

CHAPTER 4

Banking and Savings

Since post-Depression deposits have been insured against bank failure by the U.S. government, Americans have pulled their money back out of cookie jars and put much of it into various financial institutions. These organizations provide places to deposit money for safekeeping, for check drafting convenience and for earning interest on certain types of accounts. In return for these and other services, the institution has the use of the money for loans and investments.

COMMERCIAL BANKS

Commercial banks offer the widest range of services among financial institutions. They handle savings and checking accounts, make a wide range of short- and long-term loans for personal and business use, and many provide estate and investment services.

Savings accounts are considered *demand deposits.* A depositor has the right to demand or to withdraw, any or all of his funds at any time during regular banking hours. Savings accounts bear interest, which is noted, along with deposits and withdrawals, in a passbook, or savings account book. To withdraw money from an account, a depositor visits his or her bank and prepares a withdrawal slip. After proper identification of the depositor and updating of the passbook, the depositor receives the money. A money market savings account pays a higher rate of interest, but requires a certain minimum balance.

Checking accounts are also demand deposits, but they allow the depositor to draw checks payable to anyone. Although checking accounts historically have not paid interest, and, in fact, have often had fees charged for that service, there has been a recent change in paying interest on NOW and Super NOW accounts.

Certificates of deposit and *money market certificates* are *time deposits.* The customer agrees to leave his money in the bank for a certain period of time—for example, two years. During this two-year period, the depositor may not withdraw the funds without incurring significant interest penalties. In return for this long-term use of the depositor's money, the bank pays a higher rate of interest.

Any of the above accounts may be established in the name of a single depositor or may be owned jointly by several depositors with right of survivorship. With joint ownership, the account belongs to the survivors upon the death of one of the co-owners.

Factors that affect your interest return are the bank's methods of compounding interest and of crediting funds entered and withdrawn during the quarter. For many years it was usual for banks to compound interest on a quarterly basis. Now, many banks compound interest daily in order to maximize the return they offer.

As for the methods of crediting funds in your account, you should know whether the bank considers the first funds you deposit to be the first withdrawn (called FIFO—first in, first out), or if the last deposits are the first withdrawn (LIFO), or if your interest is paid on your low balance of the quarter. Without going into great detail, it is noteworthy that LIFO and a method called "day of deposit, day of withdrawal" (DD/DW) offer advantages to the depositor. Low balance and FIFO accounting methods may provide less interest on otherwise identical accounts, depending upon the activity in the account during the quarter.

Most banks insure their deposits through the Federal Deposit Insurance Corporation (FDIC). This governmental agency was established to protect people from losing their deposited assets if a bank fails. The amount of coverage is established by law. Be sure your bank provides this insurance and check the coverage limits. Accounts can be established in several name combinations (for example, husband alone, husband and wife, wife alone, husband and child, etc.) or, if necessary, in several banks to have all of your funds insured.

MUTUAL SAVINGS BANKS

Mutual savings banks are chartered in fewer than half of the states, mostly in the Northeast, and maintain about one-fifth of the nation's savings funds. These banks specialize in mortgage and home improvement loans. Until the federal regulations expire, mutual savings banks are allowed by law to pay a somewhat higher interest rate on savings accounts than commercial banks.

SAVINGS AND LOAN ASSOCIATIONS

A savings and loan association, or building and loan association, is a group of people who have pooled their funds in order to lend money. The money is primarily loaned for home buying and building and for other construction purposes. The funds may be loaned to other members of the organization, or to nonmembers.

Each investor in an S&L, as they are called, is issued a number of shares in the organization, according to the amount of money invested. The dividends earned by shareholders in S&Ls are similar to interest earned by depositors in a bank. Most savings and loan associations also have their shares insured by the Federal Deposit Insurance Corporation (FDIC).

The S&Ls provide, basically, the same accounts as a commercial bank.

CREDIT UNIONS

A credit union is similar in nature and function to a savings and loan association. Credit union members, though, have some common bond for membership—they are employees of the same company, members of the same church, labor union, farm group, etc. Members put their money into "share accounts" and receive shares in the union. The funds are used to make short-term loans to the membership.

Most credit unions honor drafts of their members. These are similar to bank checks.

SAFE-DEPOSIT BOXES

Safe-deposit boxes provide a place for the storage of valuables at a small cost. Most banks rent safe-deposit boxes. There are also a few safe-deposit companies that provide this service as their only business.

Safe-deposit boxes come in various sizes which determine the rental price. For a nominal fee, stocks, bonds, wills, deeds, gold, silver and other valuables can be protected from both burglary and fire. Even though this book provides document pockets for keeping valuable papers and documents, it is suggested that originals be kept in a safe-deposit box and that copies, for easy reference, be kept in this book.

When you rent a safe-deposit box, you are given a key. When you wish access to the box, both your key and a bank key must be used simultaneously. Neither key, alone, will open the box.

For further protection, you must sign a slip each time you seek access to the box. Your signature is compared to the signature placed on file at the time of the box rental.

The safe-deposit box, like a bank account, may be owned in a single name or jointly. Joint ownership allows access by someone else if you are prevented by sickness or absence, from getting into the box. In addition, joint ownership will allow access to the box by your co-owners after your death. Most states require the depository to seal the box upon learning of the death of a co-owner. However, it can be opened by a surviving co-owner in the presence of a state official, who inventories the assets and delivers the inventory to the probate court. This assures that the assets of the decedent will be properly reported to the court and that the applicable inheritance taxes will be applied to the contents of the box.

It is most important that someone know where the key to the box is located. The forms at the end of this chapter provide a place for you to give that information. You may keep your key in an envelope in Document Pocket #5, if you wish.

BANKING AND SAVINGS

Accounts and Safe-Deposit Boxes

Types of Accounts:

　　　S = *Savings Account*　　　C = *Checking Account*　　　CD = *Certificate of Deposit*
　　　　　　　　　MMC = *Money Market Certificate*

(The above abbreviations may be used alone or in combination to describe different types of bank accounts or safe-deposit boxes.)

☐ I have no bank accounts or safe-deposit boxes.

☐ I have the following bank accounts or safe-deposit boxes:

Name of institution: _____

Address: _____

_____

Account #: _____　　　Type: _____　　　Owner(s): _____

Account #: _____　　　Type: _____　　　Owner(s): _____

Account #: _____　　　Type: _____　　　Owner(s): _____

Safe-deposit box: _____　　　Key is located: _____

❖❖❖❖❖❖

Name of institution: _____

Address: _____

_____

Account #: _____　　　Type: _____　　　Owner(s): _____

Account #: _____　　　Type: _____　　　Owner(s): _____

Account #: _____　　　Type: _____　　　Owner(s): _____

Safe-deposit box: _____　　　Key is located: _____

❖❖❖❖❖❖

Name of institution: _____

Address: _____

_____

Account #: _____　　　Type: _____　　　Owner(s): _____

Account #: _____　　　Type: _____　　　Owner(s): _____

Account #: _____　　　Type: _____　　　Owner(s): _____

Safe-deposit box: _____　　　Key is located: _____

BANKING AND SAVINGS

Accounts and Safe-Deposit Boxes

Types of Accounts:

S = *Savings Account*   C = *Checking Account*   CD = *Certificate of Deposit*
MMC = *Money Market Certificate*

(The above abbreviations may be used alone or in combination to describe different types of bank accounts or safe-deposit boxes.)

☐ I have no bank accounts or safe-deposit boxes.

☐ I have the following bank accounts or safe-deposit boxes:

Name of institution: _____

Address: _____

_____

Account #: _____ Type: _____ Owner(s): _____

Account #: _____ Type: _____ Owner(s): _____

Account #: _____ Type: _____ Owner(s): _____

Safe-deposit box: _____ Key is located: _____

❖❖❖❖❖❖

Name of institution: _____

Address: _____

_____

Account #: _____ Type: _____ Owner(s): _____

Account #: _____ Type: _____ Owner(s): _____

Account #: _____ Type: _____ Owner(s): _____

Safe-deposit box: _____ Key is located: _____

❖❖❖❖❖❖

Name of institution: _____

Address: _____

_____

Account #: _____ Type: _____ Owner(s): _____

Account #: _____ Type: _____ Owner(s): _____

Account #: _____ Type: _____ Owner(s): _____

Safe-deposit box: _____ Key is located: _____

BANKING AND SAVINGS

Safe-Deposit Box Inventories

Safe-deposit box # _____ inventory: Safe-deposit box # _____ inventory:

_____   _____

_____   _____

_____   _____

_____   _____

_____   _____

_____   _____

_____   _____

_____   _____

_____   _____

_____   _____

_____   _____

_____   _____

_____   _____

_____   _____

_____   _____

_____   _____

_____   _____

_____   _____

_____   _____

_____   _____

_____   _____

CHAPTER 5

Securities

The term *securities,* as used in this book, refers to the types of investments commonly traded on various stock exchanges or in the over-the-counter market. They are normally handled through a stockbroker. Current exchange methods allow an investor to complete transactions almost instantaneously, making the purchase and sale of such securities a simple procedure.

STOCKS

A share of stock represents one unit of ownership in a corporation. Naturally, the percentage of ownership represented by one share of stock will depend on the number of shares issued by the corporation. If only 100 shares of stock are issued, one share represents a one percent ownership interest in the corporation. If millions of shares are issued, one share of stock represents only a miniscule ownership interest.

Common stock is the basic corporate stock. If the corporation issues no other types of stock, common stock represents the entire corporate ownership. If a corporation were to dissolve, the assets (after payment of debts) would be distributed to the common stockholders in proportion to the number of shares they hold. The common stockholders have the right to manage the affairs of the corporation through a board of directors, which they elect.

Preferred stock, as its name implies, has certain preferences over common stock. Many corporations do not have preferred stock. It may be established in the corporate charter when the corporation is formed, or later added to the charter by the majority action of the common stockholders.

The preferences, or priorities, given to preferred stocks are not identical within different corporations, but are spelled out in the individual corporate charters. The most usual preference enjoyed by the preferred stockholder is a priority in the distribution of profits. For example, preferred stockholders may be entitled to a fixed dividend before any dividends can be paid to common stockholders. Although this is often the only priority given to preferred stockholders, some have a preference over common stockholders in the distribution of assets when a corporation dissolves. If that is the case, the preferred stockholder is completely paid off before any distribution is made to the common stockholders.

In order to gain these preferences, preferred stockholders lose certain rights. For example, they usually do not have the right to vote for the election of the management team nor the right to share in corporate profits for any more than their fixed preferential dividends.

Since the return remains constant, the price fluctuations of preferred stock more closely resemble the price changes of corporate bonds than of common stock.

BONDS AND DEBENTURES

Most corporations need to borrow money from time to time. This may be due to cyclical money shortages, plans to expand facilities, to develop new products or for any number of other reasons. Money may either be borrowed from a lending institution, or the corporation may sell a series of bonds to investment bankers (called "underwriters"), who in turn sell the bonds to investors.

Various types of bonds are issued by corporations. The simplest form of a bond is called a *debenture.* It is a form of promissory note secured only by the corporation's financial ability to pay it when it becomes due. Along with preferred stocks, debentures are sometimes referred to as the "senior securities" of the corporation. They are entitled to interest payments before any dividends are paid on common stock, and they stand ahead of common stock in the distribution of capital if the corporation is dissolved.

When a corporation issues *mortgage bonds,* it uses certain designated assets of the corporation as security. If the company is unable to pay off the bonds when they become due, the bond holders have a priority claim against those assets. The corporation may also secure an issue of bonds by depositing certain collateral (usually stocks, bonds, etc.) with a trustee. A bond secured in this manner is called a *collateral trust bond.*

Income bonds promise to repay the principal on a designated date, but agree to pay interest only if the corporate earnings are sufficient.

Municipal bonds are issued by a state, county, city, bridge authority or other political subdivision. Normally, they have the added advantage of being free from U.S. federal income tax liability. This produces a large market in "municipals."

We normally think of a bond as being in the face amount of $1,000. However, many bonds are issued for larger or smaller amounts. Interest rates vary greatly. Some bonds may carry interest as low as 1½ percent or 2 percent, while other bonds may bring 15 percent or more. Since the interest rate on a bond is fixed at the time of its issue, the salable value of the bond will rise or fall depending on the actual rate of interest offered in the financial community. If the going interest rate is 9 percent, a $1,000 bond bearing 6 percent interest will not find a market and will have to sell for less. In reverse, if the bond bears a higher interest rate than the current rate in the financial community, it may sell for a premium.

The price of municipal and corporate bonds appearing in your newspaper reflects a percent of the face value of the bond. For example, if the face value of the bond is $1,000, a quotation of 95 means that the bond is being sold for $950. On the other hand, a quotation of 104 means the bond is being sold for $1,040. Quotations on government bonds are in decimals with the figures after the decimal point representing, curiously enough, 32nds of a dollar. A quote of 96.16 is equivalent to 96 16/32nds, or 96½, which would mean a bond with a face value of $1,000 would sell for $965.

MUTUAL FUNDS

Since some individuals do not have the confidence, the necessary "know-how," nor the desire to learn to invest their money themselves, *mutual funds* have been developed. A mutual fund acquires a portfolio of securities through the mass purchasing power of many individuals. It is managed by professionals. By selecting a mutual fund that purchases investments designed for your particular investment objectives, you get the benefits of professional management.

Many types of mutual funds are available. They may invest in common stocks specifically for income, growth or speculative purposes. Other funds limit their purchases to municipal bonds.

Regardless of the type of mutual fund chosen, you should know that certain funds are sold by stockbrokers or salespersons and that there is an initial charge or "load" for advising you and acting as your agent. On the other hand, "no-load" mutual funds are available through direct mailings and magazine and newspaper advertisements. A "management fee" is charged annually. This fee is usually larger for the "no-load" funds. If both "load" and "no-load" funds are held for a few years, the total cost to the investor is about the same.

MONEY MARKET FUNDS

A *money market fund* is similar to a mutual fund in that the individual's investment is combined with other investments in order to create a large fund of money, which is invested in commercial paper, certificates of deposit and other short-term securities bearing high interest rates. Normally, the earnings are determined daily and interest continuously added to the investor's account. No specific rate of interest is provided (as contrasted to a bond), and the earnings fluctuate with the performance of investments in the fund. The short maturity and diversity of investment is such that, normally, there is little fluctuation in earnings over a six-month period. However, the investor should continually check the performance of the fund so that money may be withdrawn if it appears that a change of investment would be advantageous.

Money market funds may be considered a parking place for money awaiting permanent investment. They provide relative safety of principal and a fairly high return of interest.

COMMODITIES

The commodities market is based upon the paper sale, or purchase, of gold, pork bellies, corn, wheat or other tangible goods for delivery on a specified date in the future. For example, if you agree to deliver a certain quantity of pork bellies in six months for $1,000, and in six months the price has dropped to $920 for that quantity, you can pick them up for $920 and deliver them at an $80 profit. If the price rises during those six months, though, you lose money.

Dealing in commodity futures is too highly speculative for the average investor. Although transactions require relatively small down payments, large profits or losses can occur. Regardless how thoroughly familiar you are with the commodities market, any investments in commodities should be regarded as very speculative.

STOCKBROKERS

Stockbrokers are in the business of handling your securities investments. You can expect them to work with you to obtain your own investment objectives—current income, long-term growth, preservation of capital or a combination of these. They act as your agent to buy, or sell, stocks and bonds and to provide records of purchases and sales. They give you the benefit of their knowledge of investments. For these services, you pay a fee based on the size of the transaction.

A reliable stockbroker is an invaluable ally to help you acquire and manage your investment portfolio. Unless you have the time and ability to scrutinize the performance of the many corporations on the market, you will generally be much better off to rely on the advice of the stockbroker. Large brokerage houses have staffs that analyze the performance and potential of various stocks.

When an account with a stockbroker is established, arrangements can be made for the stocks to be retained by the brokerage. In this way, your dividends and interest are collected for you and sent to you as you wish. A small semi-annual charge is usually made for this service, but the convenience, plus the monthly and quarterly statements, are helpful in record keeping and tax preparation. They are safe, and your safe deposit box will not be cluttered.

The forms at the end of this chapter provide a convenient place for you to record information about the securities you own, where they are located, and the name and address of your broker. Keep the listing of securities up to date. When you add or delete securities from the list, or even when you review the list, erase the date at the bottom of the page and insert the new date.

SECURITIES

Stocks, Bonds, Debentures and Mutual Funds

☐ I do not own any securities (stocks, bonds, debentures, mutual funds, etc.)

☐ I owned the securities listed on the next page as of the date the page was last revised.

☐ I have used the following brokerage firms for the purchase and sale of securities:

Brokerage Firm #1

Name of firm: _____ Branch: _____

Address: _____ Telephone #: _____

_____

_____

Account #: _____ Account executive: _____

Brokerage Firm #2

Name of firm: _____ Branch: _____

Address: _____ Telephone #: _____

_____

_____

Account #: _____ Account executive: _____

Brokerage Firm #3

Name of firm: _____ Branch: _____

Address: _____ Telephone #: _____

_____

_____

Account #: _____ Account executive: _____

Circle "All of" or "Part of" where appropriate.

☐ **All of / Part of** my securities are kept in my safe-deposit box.

☐ **All of / Part of** my securities are kept by ☐ Brokerage #1 ☐ Brokerage #2 ☐ Brokerage #3

☐ **All of / Part of** my securities are located: _____

SECURITIES

Stocks, Bonds, Debentures and Mutual Funds

C = *Common stock*   P = *Preferred stock*   M = *Mutual fund*   B = *Bond*   D = *Debenture*   MMF = *Money Market funds*

(The above abbreviations may be used to describe the different types of securities you have invested in.)

☐ I have not invested in any securities.   ☐ I have invested in the following securities:

Company	Type of Security	Number of Shares	Date of Purchase	Total Cost	Unit Cost	Adjustment to Unit Cost (Explain)

The above list of securities was last reviewed, or revised, by me on: _____
Date

SECURITIES

Stocks, Bonds, Debentures and Mutual Funds

C = *Common stock*   P = *Preferred stock*   M = *Mutual fund*   B = *Bond*   D = *Debenture*   MMF = *Money Market funds*

(The above abbreviations may be used to describe the different types of securities you have invested in.)

☐ I have not invested in any securities.   ☐ I have invested in the following securities:

Company	Type of Security	Number of Shares	Date of Purchase	Total Cost	Unit Cost	Adjustment to Unit Cost (Explain)

The above list of securities was last reviewed, or revised, by me on: _____
                                                                          Date

SECURITIES

Stocks, Bonds, Debentures and Mutual Funds

C = *Common stock*   P = *Preferred stock*   M = *Mutual fund*   B = *Bond*   D = *Debenture*   MMF = *Money Market funds*

(The above abbreviations may be used to describe the different types of securities you have invested in.)

☐ I have not invested in any securities.   ☐ I have invested in the following securities:

Company	Type of Security	Number of Shares	Date of Purchase	Total Cost	Unit Cost	Adjustment to Unit Cost (Explain)

The above list of securities was last reviewed, or revised, by me on: _____
Date

CHAPTER 6

Real Estate

Real estate (or real property) is land and everything permanently attached to the land. A person buying real estate not only purchases soil, but the trees, shrubs, fences and buildings secured to it. Your house is real estate.

OWNERSHIP INTERESTS IN REAL ESTATE

The largest ownership interest available in land is called a *fee simple estate.* It provides the owner with complete control over the land—subject, of course, to zoning laws, chain of title restrictions, use of the land so that it does not interfere with adjoining property owners, etc. A fee simple estate is the type of ownership interest that is normally purchased and sold on the open market. Its name dates back to the early common law of England.

Although the common law provided for other types of estates, or interests, in land (fee simple conditional, fee tail, etc.), the only other commonly used ownership interest is the *life estate.* A life estate, created by deed or by will, gives a person the right to the use of the property during that person's lifetime, or during the term of some other person's life. A son, for example, may deed his mother a life estate to a home. This would ensure that the mother has a place to live during her lifetime. However, upon her death, the full ownership of the property would revert to the son.

Real estate may be owned by one or by several individuals. If an individual is deeded a fee simple estate to the land, he or she has acquired the full ownership interest. That individual alone has the right to sell the real estate, transfer it by will, rent it, or use it in any other legal way.

When a fee simple estate is acquired by more than one individual, however, the deed establishes whether they are *joint owners* or *common owners.* Many sorts of property may be owned through these types of ownership—automobiles, stocks, bank accounts, real estate, etc.—and there are distinct differences between the two.

With both joint and common ownership, the owners have equal rights to use and enjoy the property during their lifetimes. Joint ownership, however, includes the *right of survivorship.* When a joint owner dies, the ownership of the property remains with the surviving owner(s). The last surviving joint owner ends up as the sole owner of the property. Another feature of joint ownership is that an owner cannot sell his interest unless the other joint owner(s) join in the sale.

It is common for husband and wife to own real estate jointly as survivorship property. This avoids the necessity of probating the real estate when the first member of the marriage dies. However, survivorship property in real estate (as well as in bank accounts, etc.) could defeat the purpose of a tax saving estate plan. Before entering into any survivorship property arrangement, discuss it with your estate planner.

A surviving parent sometimes attempts to avoid probate costs by establishing joint ownership of real estate with his children. This can create a number of problems (see Chapter 8) and is not normally recommended.

With common ownership, each person owns an undivided interest in the whole property, but there is no survivorship feature. Each of the owners may sell his or her undivided interest or may will it on his or her death to anyone. When friends join together to purchase resort property for general use by their families, they often take title as common owners. If one of the owners dies, that owner's estate, or heirs, would own his or her undivided interest in the real estate.

In California and a few other states, property acquired during marriage automatically becomes community property, so long as the spouses have no agreement to the contrary. Each spouse owns a 50 percent interest in all such property (unless it can be shown that the property was acquired exclusively through the means of one spouse from before the marriage). As with common ownership, each spouse has the right to assign by will the ownership of their portion of community property. If you live in a community property State, this will affect the property over which you have control in your will.

SPECIAL USE VALUATION

Real estate is usually valued for federal estate tax purposes at its fair market value, based on its highest and best use. This could be a figure substantially higher than its fair market value for farming or business purposes—its use at the time of your death. And, of course, the higher the estate value, the higher the estate tax.

Your personal representative or executor may have the right to elect to value the real estate on the basis of the lower value. However, certain tests must be met. These tests are primarily concerned with ownership and land usage at the time of your death, to whom you leave the land, how long you have been using it for farming or business, etc.

If the above facts may apply to you, see your tax or estate adviser.

The forms in this chapter provide a place for you to list your ownership interests in real estate. It is not necessary to give the legal description of the real estate as it appears on the deed, but the land should be sufficiently identified so that it can be easily located. The deed by which you took title should be recorded at the county seat to give notice of your ownership interest in the land. After the deed has been copied by the county office, it can be placed in Document Pocket #6.

OWNERSHIP INTERESTS

My Real Estate

CM = Commercial   CO = Condominium   F = Farm land   I = Investment property
O = Other (describe)   R = Residence   V = Vacant land
(The above abbreviations may be used alone or in combination to describe different types of real estate.)

☐ I have no ownership interest in any real estate.

☐ I have an ownership interest in the following real estate:

Street address: _____

in the _____ of _____
        Specify whether city or township   *Name of city or township*

County of _____ State of _____

Type of real estate: _____

My ownership interest is ☐ sole, ☐ community property, ☐ joint with right of survivorship

with: _____

_____

or ☐ as a tenant in common with: _____

I acquired my ownership interest on or about: _____

My ownership interest became joint with right of survivorship on or about: _____

Purchase price of real estate: _____

I owe money on the real estate to:

    Name: _____

    Address: _____

    _____

On or about: _____ , I sold my ownership interest to:

    Name: _____

    Address: _____

    _____

for the sum of $ _____ , and I receive the sum of $ _____
per month from the sale price.

The deed, land contract, mortgage, purchase information, sale information, etc., are located:

_____

OWNERSHIP INTERESTS

My Real Estate

CM = Commercial   *CO = Condominium*   *F = Farm land*   *I = Investment property*
       O = Other (describe)   *R = Residence*   *V = Vacant land*
(The above abbreviations may be used alone or in combination to describe different types of real estate.)

Street address: _____

in the _____ of _____
              Specify whether city or township   *Name of city or township*

County of _____ State of _____

Type of real estate: _____

My ownership interest is ☐ sole, ☐ community property, ☐ joint with right of survivorship

with: _____

_____

or ☐ as a tenant in common with: _____

I acquired my ownership interest on or about: _____

My ownership interest became joint with right of survivorship on or about: _____

Purchase price of real estate: _____

I owe money on the real estate to:

   Name: _____

   Address: _____

   _____

On or about: _____ , I sold my ownership interest to:

   Name: _____

   Address: _____

   _____

for the sum of $ _____ , and I receive the sum of $ _____
per month from the sale price.

The deed, land contract, mortgage, purchase information, sale information, etc., are located:

_____

OWNERSHIP INTERESTS

My Real Estate

CM = Commercial   *CO = Condominium*   *F = Farm land*   *I = Investment property*

O = Other (describe)   *R = Residence*   *V = Vacant land*

(The above abbreviations may be used alone or in combination to describe different types of real estate.)

Street address: _____

in the _____ of _____
      Specify whether city or township   Name of city or township

County of _____ State of _____

Type of real estate: _____

My ownership interest is ☐ sole, ☐ community property, ☐ joint with right of survivorship

with: _____

_____

or ☐ as a tenant in common with: _____

I acquired my ownership interest on or about: _____

My ownership interest became joint with right of survivorship on or about: _____

Purchase price of real estate: _____

I owe money on the real estate to:

Name: _____

Address: _____

_____

On or about: _____ , I sold my ownership interest to:

Name: _____

Address: _____

_____

for the sum of $ _____ , and I receive the sum of $ _____
per month from the sale price.

The deed, land contract, mortgage, purchase information, sale information, etc., are located:

_____

CHAPTER 7

Miscellaneous Assets and Debts

The preceding chapters provided forms for you to list your checking and savings accounts, life insurance, liability insurance, stocks, bonds, real estate, etc. This chapter is included to provide you with forms to list your miscellaneous assets and debts.

ASSETS

Since forms cannot be tailor-made to cover the assets of everyone, this section provides a place to list a number of common assets—motor vehicles, names and addresses of debtors, business interests, whether you are beneficiary of a trust, whether you have an interest in a trust or real estate at the death of another person and information regarding any claims or lawsuits you may have against other persons.

Additional space is provided for you to list any other assets of value. Normally, it should not be necessary to list your household furnishings, since they are out in the open for your heirs to see. However, if some item of furniture has great value because of its antiquity, list it. The same applies to expensive paintings, coin or stamp collections, valuable jewelry, etc.

Have you loaned furniture to a friend, relative or to your office? Are any of the furnishings in your home borrowed from a friend? Have you already given an item to someone even though the item is still in your possession?

If there is any question as to whether a particular item should be listed, list it.

DEBTS

It is likely your heirs will have no knowledge of your debts. Naturally, you should not take time to list monthly bills. But if you have borrowed money from a relative, friend or associate, tell your heirs about it. If someone has started a lawsuit against you, describe it and record the name of your lawyer.

ASSETS

Personal Property

☐ I own the following motor vehicles:

Year	Description	Balance Owed to:

The titles for the above vehicles are located: _____

_____

The following persons owe me money:

Name of debtor	Address	Amount

☐ I have the following miscellaneous assets, which might be difficult for my heirs to locate, or which might not be recognized as having significant value:

Description	Location	Significance	Estimated Value

(Any of the above may be continued on page 126.)

ASSETS

Business Interests

☐ I have no ownership interest in any business.

☐ I have an interest in the following businesses:

Business name: _____ Type of business: _____

Address: _____ % of ownership: _____

Partner(s): _____ % of ownership: _____

_____ _____

_____ _____

❖❖❖❖❖

Business name: _____ Type of business: _____

Address: _____ % of ownership: _____

Partner(s): _____ % of ownership: _____

_____ _____

_____ _____

❖❖❖❖❖

Business name: _____ Type of business: _____

Address: _____ % of ownership: _____

Partner(s): _____ % of ownership: _____

_____ _____

_____ _____

❖❖❖❖❖

☐ I have an interest in the following patents and/or copyrights:

Description	Pending?	Date Granted	Patent or Copyright Number	Termination Date

(Any of the above may be continued on page 126.)

ASSETS

Legal Action and Trusts

☐ I have a possible claim (personal injury, breach of contract, etc.) against:

Name: _____

Address: _____

_____

Description: _____

☐ I have a lawsuit pending against:

Name: _____

Address: _____

_____

☐ I have an uncollected legal judgment against:

Name: _____

Address: _____

_____

If you are not represented in the above by the lawyer listed in "Professional Advisers," page 156, list your lawyer's name and address here:

Lawyer's name: _____

Address: _____

_____

❖❖❖❖❖

☐ I am the beneficiary of a trust.

Description: _____

Trustee: _____

☐ I am entitled to a remainder interest in a trust or in real estate at the death of:

_____

Description: _____

Trustee (if applicable): _____

(Any of the above may be continued on page 126.)

DEBTS

☐ I owe the following debts, which have not been previously mentioned:
(Personal loans, notes, etc., and NOT normal monthly bills, etc.)

To Whom	Address	What for	Amount

❖❖❖❖❖❖

☐ I may be subject to a claim against me by: _____

Description: _____

☐ I have a pending lawsuit against me by: _____

Description: _____

☐ I have an unpaid legal judgment against me in favor of: _____

_____

Description: _____

☐ I have the following miscellaneous obligations or debts:

Description: _____

_____

_____

_____

(Any of the following may be continued on reverse.)

ASSETS AND DEBTS

Miscellaneous Assets and Debts

_____

_____

_____

_____

_____

_____

_____

_____

_____

_____

_____

_____

_____

_____

_____

_____

_____

_____

_____

_____

_____

_____

_____

_____

_____

CHAPTER 8

Will, Trust Agreements, Etc.

The word *estate* brings to mind mansions, objets d'art, chauffeur-driven automobiles and *money.* But do not be fooled. Anyone with a home, car, bank account, clothes, investments, or even the inherited gold watch from Granddad, has an estate. Your "estate" is the sum total of everything you own.

When a person dies, estate's assets are determined, the funeral expenses and other debts are paid, inheritance and estate taxes are settled and any monies owed to the person are collected. After that, the remainder is distributed according to the directions expressed in the person's will. If there is no will, the assets are distributed according to the laws of the state in which the person lived. One who leaves a will is said to have died "testate" (leaving a Testament—another word for will). A person who does not leave a will is said to have died "intestate" (without leaving a testament).

PROBATE

Probate is the term used for the legal procedure established by each state, which leads to the estate's final distribution. The probate of an estate is supervised by a special court usually known as a probate court, or, in some states, a surrogate court or orphan's court.

Many believe that it is not necessary for an estate to be probated if the person who died, the *decedent,* has left a will. This is not true. Some legal authority must determine its validity, identify the heirs, pass judgment on claims against the estate, calculate the amount of death taxes to be paid and distribute the remaining assets to the proper persons. Except for determining the validity of the will, the same procedure is followed for someone who dies intestate.

Filing fees, advertising expenses, appraiser's fees, etc., are minor costs in probating an estate. The major costs are attorney fees and fees for the personal representative charged with the management of the estate.

EXECUTORS AND ADMINISTRATORS

If the decedent left a will, the estate's *personal representative* may be called an *executor,* since that person "executes" the provisions of the Will. An intestate estate is "administered" by an *administrator.* The duties are identical; only the titles differ.

The personal representative is responsible for a number of tasks. He or she must collect the assets of the decedent; have them appraised; liquidate them to pay debts or to make distribution to heirs; pay the proper claims against the estate; prepare final income tax returns for the decedent; prepare state and federal inheritance and estate tax returns; distribute the remaining assets according to the terms of the will or the intestate laws of the state; record the necessary papers to clear title to real estate; and obtain receipts from the beneficiaries. After the receipts have been filed, the personal representative is discharged by the probate court.

The attorney for the estate guides the personal representative, prepares all legal petitions, orders, etc., and makes certain that the probate proceedings are proper.

In many states, compensation for the personal representative is set as a percentage of the inventory value of the estate. This fee is usually based upon a sliding scale. As the size of the estate increases, a smaller percentage is taken from the greater portions of the estate. For example, a personal representative might be entitled to a fee of 5 percent of the first $5,000 of an estate, 4 percent of the next $10,000, 3 percent of the next $35,000 and 2 percent of anything over $50,000.

Other states do not use a percentage figure but set the compensation in an amount that a probate judge has decided to be "just and reasonable." There can be a great difference in the amount of work involved by two personal representatives, even though each of the estates has a value of $100,000. Clearly it would be much simpler to administer an estate consisting of $100,000 cash, with no claims against it, than to administer an estate of $100,000 with real estate, stocks, bonds, and having many debts that must be investigated and paid. Completion of the forms in this book could save fees in the probating of your estate.

LOCAL ESTATE AND INHERITANCE TAXES

As part of the probate procedure, the personal representative of the estate must pay all estate and inheritance taxes due to the state and federal governments. Almost all of the states in the U.S. have some type of death tax—either an inheritance tax or an estate tax. An "inheritance tax" is based upon the amount of *inheritance* received by each beneficiary. An "estate tax" is imposed on the total size of the *estate*, regardless of the size of the individual inheritances.

Before calculating the amount of an inheritance tax or an estate tax, the laws usually provide that funeral expenses, valid debts and lawful expenses of administering the estate may first be deducted. In addition, the tax rates and exemptions imposed on different beneficiaries may vary depending on their kinship to the decedent. For example, a spouse may have a total exemption on an inheritance. Parents, children and grand-children may have an exemption of $10,000. However, nieces, nephews, aunts, uncles, cousins and nonrelatives may have no exemption. Then, for example, spouses, children, parents and grandchildren may pay a rate of 2 percent on the first $50,000 inherited, 4 percent on the next $100,000, 6 percent on the next $300,000, etc. At the same time, all other persons may be taxed at 10 percent on the first $50,000, 12 percent on the next $100,000, and so forth. Usually, charitable gifts are not taxed so long as the recipient qualifies as a true, charitable organization.

With estate taxes, just like most income taxes, the lowest rate is applied to the bottom portion of an estate. As an estate rises in value, the tax rate increases, in stairstep percentages, on the higher values.

The "taxable estate" may not be the same as the inventory value of assets set by the probate court. For example, even though jointly owned property is neither probated nor generally subject to state death taxes, it is considered to be part of the "taxable estate" for federal estate tax purposes. Life insurance proceeds and almost any asset that passes to another individual at death are also subject to federal estate taxes, regardless of whether the state requires probate of those assets.

In a sizable estate, the federal estate tax can be very expensive. There are ways to minimize the taxes imposed upon your estate. *See a good estate planner.* If you do not know one, talk to your lawyer. If your attorney has the background to plan your estate, he or she will. If not, he or she can refer you to a qualified person.

UNIFIED FEDERAL GIFT AND ESTATE TAX CREDIT

A person who makes a gift (a donor) is subject to the federal gift tax. However, not all gifts are taxable. Each donor is entitled to a $10,000 annual exclusion on gifts to each recipient. In other words, a donor can give $10,000 to as many different persons or organizations as desired without being subject to gift tax. So long as you do not exceed your exclusions, you do not need to file a gift tax return. However, to have your gifts considered made one-half by you and one-half by your spouse, your spouse must sign the consent *on the gift tax return.*

You do not have to file a gift tax return to report gifts to your spouse regardless of the amount of these gifts; however, you must file a gift tax return if your spouse is not a U.S. citizen and the total gifts made to your spouse during the year exceeded $100,000. A few other exceptions exist pertaining to gifts of a terminable interest and the need to file a return to make a Qualified Terminal Interest Property (Q/TIP) election, etc. (See your tax adviser.)

You must file an annual return for gifts exceeding the exclusions. The amount of gift tax is determined and applied against your lifetime unified tax credit of $192,800, which is applicable to the combined total of gift tax and estate tax at your death—and is equivalent to a combined taxable estate plus taxable gifts totaling $600,000.

A form has been provided for you to keep a record of your taxable gifts for your personal representative.

THE WILL

In Merrie Olde England, a person had little control over the manner in which his estate was divided. Distribution was generally determined by British law, which generously rewarded the first-born son to the virtual exclusion of other children. It was not until 1540 that the first Statute of Wills gave a person the right to decide, to some extent, how his property should be distributed after his death.

To prevent forgeries, fraud and undue influence, each state has prescribed the method for a will to be executed. Although the requirements are relatively simple, they must be strictly followed or the will is not valid. The state provides that the will must be identified as such by the signer to a certain number of witnesses. Then, usually, the signer and the witnesses must sign the will in the presence of each other. Unfortunately, many people attempt to prepare their own wills without being aware of the formal requirements of execution. This may result in an invalid will.

It is not worthwhile to save money by preparing your own will. See your attorney! Discuss the cost of a will and shop around, if necessary, for a fee with which you feel comfortable. An attorney should be able to prepare a simple will for a modest fee. An attorney not only knows the formal requirements for the execution of the will, but will be able to set out your desires clearly, minimizing the chance of some disgruntled individual contesting the validity of the will.

The laws of some states recognize that there can be circumstances in which an individual may not have time to arrange for a proper will. For example, a soldier dying on the field of battle would have no opportunity to prepare and execute a will. In circumstances of impending death, some states will allow an oral (nuncupative) will. Don't rely on this! In addition, some states allow an unwitnessed will that is entirely in the handwriting of the testator (a holographic will). Don't rely on this either!

A will allows you to designate the beneficiaries of your estate. Generally, a man who leaves a valid will in effect at his death (a testator) cannot exclude his wife. If he does, the wife has a right to "take against the will" and receive a certain percentage (up to 100 percent) of the amount she would have received had there been no will. In response to the changing view of women in society, some states have enacted similar provisions to protect the husband from exclusion by the wife's will. Except for the limitations involving a spouse, a testator can generally leave his or her estate to anyone.

By will, a person may, among other things, designate a personal representative; decide whether adopted grandchildren will inherit in the same manner as natural grandchildren; appoint a guardian of any minor children; and create a trust.

TRUST AGREEMENTS

A trust can be established in a will (called a "testamentary trust") to accomplish many different ends. For example, a testator may have raised two of her children, at her expense, through a full college education. She may, however, have a young child at home. If her estate were left equally to the three children, it would mean that the youngster would have to provide for his own upbringing and college education out of his one-third share of the estate. To avoid this injustice, the testator could leave her estate to a trustee (a bank or trust company, for example) for the use and benefit of all of her children. However, the trustee might be instructed that no division should be made of the estate assets until the estate had paid for the upbringing and college education of the young child. Many variations can be made in the scheme of *when* inheritances should be paid, *how* they should be paid and *under what circumstances* they should be paid. In effect, the trustee handles the estate for a certain period of time after the person's death in the manner the person has directed.

Trusts can also be used by an estate planner to help minimize the effects of estate taxation. Since this can become quite involved, discuss your particular situation with an estate planning specialist.

Besides being established by a will, trusts can also be created during the person's lifetime. The individual enters into a trust agreement with himself or herself, or with a selected trustee such as a bank. The establishment of such a trust is generally for estate planning or tax saving purposes. Such a trust (created during lifetime) is called a "living" or *inter vivos* trust.

The individual can transfer ownership of desired assets to the trustee. At the death of the individual, the trustee will distribute the remaining assets in the trust in accordance with the provisions of the trust agreement.

The inter vivos trust may be used to avoid the probating of a decedent's assets. Your estate planner can best determine whether this would fit your particular situation.

INTESTATE SUCCESSION

If you die without a will (intestate), your estate will be distributed in accordance with the laws of *intestate succession.* The laws of your state of residence will govern the distribution of all of your assets except real estate located in another state or country; and the laws of the state in which the real estate is located will determine its distribution. Whether you like it or not, that's the way it is!

All of the states have established laws to determine the manner of estate distribution for an intestate decedent. Without these laws, there would be endless family disputes over the decedent's worldly goods. (If you don't think this is true, any lawyer will vouch for the family fights that take place even under the laws of intestate succession.)

It is always possible that your state's laws of intestate succession will provide the exact method by which you wish to divide your estate. But don't count on it! Since most persons want everything to go to their spouse, it seems strange that the various legislatures did not design it that way. In most instances, the surviving spouse will receive 50 percent of the estate if there is one surviving child and 33⅓ percent of the estate if there are two or more surviving children. On the other hand, if there are no surviving children, the spouse normally gets 50 percent and the parents of the decedent get 50 percent. If something like this is what you want, check the laws of intestate succession in the state in which you reside and in any other state in which you own real estate, and sit back and do nothing. On the other hand, if you want your assets specifically distributed according to your wishes, have your attorney prepare a will that reflects those wishes.

JOINTLY OWNED PROPERTY

The intestate succession laws or directions of your will affect only property that *you* own at the time of your death. Many people own real estate, bank accounts, automobiles, etc., in joint names, with right of survivorship, with their spouse or with someone else. At the death of a co-owner, joint property automatically belongs to the surviving co-owner. In other words, *joint property is not an asset of the decedent's estate.* Neither the will nor the laws of intestate succession can control the distribution of joint property. You must take this into consideration for your after-death planning.

Joint ownership offers certain advantages in estate planning. However, a total reliance on joint ownership to effect a plan of estate distribution may end up defeating the equitable distribution you had envisioned.

For example, let us suppose that your spouse dies before you, and that you have three adult children who, in turn, have children. In order to avoid probate expense (since jointly owned property does not require probate administration), it would appear simple to place your home in the names of yourself and each of your three children, jointly. Then, upon your death, the three children would be joint co-owners of the home.

Simple? Not really. Too many things can happen. Suppose child A dies shortly after your death. Now the home is owned by children B and C—to the exclusion of child A's children. Or, suppose you subsequently decide that you wish to sell the home and one of your children, for whatever reason, refuses to approve the sale. An expensive legal proceeding could force the sale, but the unwilling child might be entitled to one-fourth of the proceeds. Or suppose one of the children became mentally incompetent and could not join in a sale of the real estate. Then, although a guardian could be appointed to enter into the sale, the incompetent child's estate would have to receive one-fourth of the proceeds. Or, suppose you and your three children were killed in an automobile accident, but that child C died five minutes later than the other three co-owners. Under those circumstances, child C's estate would be the sole owner of the real estate since that child had outlived the other joint co-owners.

As stated here, there may be a definite place for joint ownership of real estate, bank accounts, etc., in your estate planning; however, be sure you know what you are doing and talk it over with your lawyer.

Remember, your will does not control jointly owned property.

YOUR WILL AND LIFE INSURANCE

The beneficiaries of your life insurance are determined by the life insurance contract between you and the insurance company. Neither your will nor the laws of intestate succession can designate to whom life insurance proceeds shall be paid. Of course, if your insurance contract designates your estate as the beneficiary of the insurance policy, the insurance company will pay the proceeds to your personal representative who, in turn, will distribute the proceeds to the estate beneficiaries.

As you can see, the execution of a will does not cover everything. But with careful planning and professional advice, you can maximize the likelihood of having your wishes carried out exactly as you expect.

THE LIVING WILL

Some individuals would prefer to die with the dignity of accepting their natural mortality than to be kept "alive" through extraordinary measures when there is little serious hope of recovery. Should this be your wish, a living will has been provided, to express your decision to your heirs, your physicians and other concerned individuals (see page 138). This is not solely for the purpose of declaring your wishes, but also to spare your survivors from facing such a decision and to offer some legal protection to medical personnel acting according to your instructions.

To make best use of your living will, sign and date it in front of two witnesses. Give copies to those concerned—your family, your family doctor, etc.—and discuss it with them. Since this may not be a legal document, it is important that those who will be carrying out your wishes be aware of and willing to carry out your decision. Look over your living will yearly, and if you have not changed your thoughts about it, initial and date it.

A living will has been prepared by The Concern For Dying Fund, 250 W. 57th Street, New York, NY 10107. Write to this nonprofit organization for forms that may be required by your state of residence.

MY WILL

General Instructions

☐ I do not have a last will and testament.

☐ I executed my last will and testament on: _____

The will was prepared by:

Name of attorney: _____

Name of law firm: _____

Address: _____
Street address and apartment number

_____
City   *State*   *ZIP code*

The will was witnessed by:

Name: _____

Address: _____
Street address and apartment number

_____
City   *State*   *ZIP code*

Further identification (neighbor, coworker, etc.): _____

Name: _____

Address: _____
Street address and apartment number

_____
City   *State*   *ZIP code*

Further identification: _____

Name: _____

Address: _____
Street address and apartment number

_____
City   *State*   *ZIP code*

Further identification: _____

MY WILL

Codicils, Trusts, Power of Attorney

Since the will was executed, I have executed _____ codicils to the will.

The codicils were executed on the following dates: _____

Name of personal representative: _____

Address: _____

_____

Name of trustee: _____

Address: _____

_____

My original will (with codicils) is located: _____

_____

and a copy is located: ☐ in Document Pocket #7, or ☐ _____

❖❖❖❖❖

☐ I have not executed a living trust agreement that is in effect at this time.

☐ I entered into a living trust agreement on _____ with:

Name of trustee: _____

Address: _____

_____

The original living trust agreement is located: _____

_____

and a copy is located: ☐ in Document Pocket #7, or ☐ _____

❖❖❖❖❖

The following person is entrusted with power of attorney:

Name: _____

Address: _____

_____

Effective date: _____   Expiration date: _____

MY WILL

Gifts

☐ I have made no gifts in excess of $10,000.

☐ I have made the following gifts in excess of $10,000:

To Whom (Donee)	Date	Gift	Value

I have filed the following federal gift tax returns:

Period Covered	Internal Revenue Office Where Filed

A LIVING WILL

To My Family, My Physician, My Lawyer And All Others Whom It May Concern

Death is as much a reality as birth, growth, and aging—it is the one certainty of life. In anticipation of decisions that may have to be made about my own dying and as an expression of my right to refuse treatment, I _____ , being of sound mind, make this statement of my wishes and instructions concerning treatment.   (print name)

By means of this document, which I intend to be legally binding, I direct my physician and other care providers, my family, and any surrogate designated by me or appointed by a court, to carry out my wishes. If I become unable, by reason of physical or mental incapacity, to make decisions about my medical care, let this document provide the guidance and authority needed to make any and all such decisions.

If I am permanently unconscious or there is no reasonable expectation of my recovery from a seriously incapacitating or lethal illness or condition, I do not wish to be kept alive by artificial means. I request that I be given all care necessary to keep me comfortable and free of pain, even if pain-relieving medications may hasten my death, and I direct that no life-sustaining treatment be provided except as I or my surrogate specifically authorize.

This request may appear to place a heavy responsibility upon you, but by making this decision according to my strong convictions, I intend to ease that burden. I am acting after careful consideration and with understanding of the consequences of your carrying out my wishes. *List optional specific provisions in the space below.*

_____ **Durable Power of Attorney for Health Care Decisions** (Cross out if you do not wish to use this section) _____

To effect my wishes, I designate _____ ,
residing at _____ (Phone #) _____ ,
(or if he or she shall for any reason fail to act, _____ (Phone #) _____ ,
residing at _____) as my health care surrogate—
that is, my attorney-in-fact regarding any and all health care decisions to be made for me, including the decision to refuse life-sustaining treatment—if I am unable to make such decisions myself. This power shall remain effective during and not be affected by my subsequent illness, disability or incapacity. My surrogate shall have authority to interpret my Living Will, and shall make decisions about my health care as specified in my instructions or, when my wishes are not clear, as the surrogate believes to be in my best interests. I release and agree to hold harmless my health care surrogate from any and all claims whatsoever arising from decisions made in good faith in the exercise of this power.

I sign this document knowingly, voluntarily, and after careful deliberation, this _____ day of _____, 19 ____.

_____
(signature)

Address _____

_____

I do hereby certify that the within document was executed and acknowledged before me by the principal this_____ day of _____, 19 _____.

_____
Notary Public

Witness_____

Printed Name _____

Address _____

_____

Witness_____

Printed Name _____

Address _____

_____

Copies of this document have been given to:

(Optional) My Living Will is registered with Concern for Dying (No. _____)
Distributed by Concern for Dying, 250 West 57th Street, New York, NY 10107 (212) 246-6962

Source: Adapted and reprinted with permission by Concern for Dying

CHAPTER 9

Final Wishes and Guide for Survivors

If you ever buried a loved one without previous discussion as to how final decisions should be made, you will remember your guilt feelings as you made the funeral arrangements. Have I spent enough on this funeral? Am I showing proper respect and love for the deceased? Should the casket be open? Would cremation be preferable? Should the body be donated for medical education?

You can spare your heirs this mental anguish by making the decisions yourself. The forms in this chapter allow you to clearly state your wishes.

When a person dies, the body must be handled in some manner. This is normally done by burial in the earth, entombment, cremation or by bequeathal of the body to a medical school. This is the first determination you must make.

Your decision may be influenced by your personal wishes, your religious background, comparative costs and other factors. For many years, cremation violated the precepts of Roman Catholicism. However, a change has taken place and many Catholics accept cremation following a religious service with the remains present. Generally speaking, Jews do not accept cremation.

It is not the purpose of this book to attempt to persuade you that one method is superior to another. If you wish to spend $25,000 on your funeral, fine. That is your business. On the other hand, if you prefer the simplicity of the least expensive method, that, too, is entirely up to you. *But tell it to your heirs!*

If you choose to have a funeral, you must decide whether it is to be public or private; whether you want an open or closed casket; who is to be the funeral director; whether you want flowers, whether you have any preference in music; who is to be the minister, priest or rabbi; whether there should be a graveside service for the commitment of your body; whether you wish memorial donations to be made to a specific organization; and whether you wish the service to be held in a church or a funeral home. There are a lot of decisions, aren't there? To make certain your preferences are known, it is best to photocopy the completed forms in this chapter and give them to your next of kin and to the funeral director or memorial society of your choice.

BURIAL AND ENTOMBMENT

Burial in the earth is, by far, the most common method in the United States of dealing with the remains. Although early Americans usually buried a body in a family or churchyard cemetery, all of the states now have regulations requiring burial in licensed cemeteries. The body is placed in a casket, lowered into the ground and covered with earth.

Caskets, or *coffins,* encase the corpse for burial purposes. They can vary from a simple pine box to an elaborate bronze coffin with an innerspring mattress. The cost of the casket will greatly affect the total charges for the funeral.

Vaults of concrete, or similar materials, are often used to surround the casket to help prevent water seepage and to prevent settling of the soil as a wooden coffin disintegrates.

Cemetery lots for earth burial may be purchased for individual caskets. Larger lots may be purchased for future use by an entire family. Most cemeteries now include in the sale price of the lot a charge for its perpetual care.

The *cost of cemetery lots* varies enormously. In urban areas costs are generally more than in rural areas because of the higher property value. Even in the same community, costs can vary widely from one cemetery to another; and indeed, substantial price differences can exist in the same cemetery. A gravesite located on a hill, for example, may be much more expensive than a cemetery lot on lower ground.

Entombment is similar to burial in the earth, except that the casket is placed in a private tomb or in a *crypt* located in a building called a *mausoleum.* Mausoleums may range from 1 to 20 stories in height. Crypts may be purchased for individual caskets or for a family of caskets.

If you choose to be buried in a cemetery or entombed in a mausoleum, you should tell your heirs where this is to take place. In other words, *select your cemetery or mausoleum.* You do not need to purchase a cemetery lot or crypt. Such a purchase is recommended, though, if you are certain that you do not intend to move from the area, or if you wish to use a specific cemetery or mausoleum regardless of future moves. Many people plan to retire to warmer climates or other desirable spots, if they can afford this luxury. If you have made a firm decision about this, purchase your lot or crypt. On the other hand, if you are not sure about your ultimate living site, merely note your preference of cemetery or mausoleum. Make sure that the cemetery of your choice allows burial without a vault, if this type of burial is your preference.

Monuments, headstones and grave markers may be used in cemeteries to identify the person buried. Monuments and headstones are generally made of stone and extend above the ground in varying heights. Grave markers are generally made of metal or stone and are placed flat on the ground. Many of the newer cemeteries require flat grave markers so that large mowing machines can operate freely. Where there are monuments or headstones, lawns must be mowed by hand—meaning higher labor costs. If you prefer a monument atop your grave, make sure that the cemetery you choose will allow it.

While you are making these decisions, you might as well determine the wording on your monument or marker. Although the majority of grave markers and monuments merely give the name of the grave occupant, the year of birth and the year of death, many monuments have epitaphs chosen by the deceased or his heirs. Note any specific directions you might have for this.

If you are a veteran of the United States military, and if your last discharge was other than dishonorable, the Veterans Administration will furnish, upon request, a headstone or marker for your unmarked grave. In addition, you, your spouse, or minor children may be buried in any National Cemetery in which space is available. (See Chapter 3, Other Benefits.)

CREMATION

Cremation is a method of disposing of a body by placing it in a special furnace which reduces it to ashes. Although fewer than 10 percent of the bodies in the United States are cremated, cremation is used widely in certain parts of the world. In fact, the word "funeral" is derived from an old word of northern India which means "smoke." Today, many people of India burn their dead on funeral pyres and scatter the ashes on the sacred river Ganges. The Vikings placed their dead in boats, set the boats afire, and sent them out to sea.

Following cremation, the ashes are returned to the heirs in a box or urn and may be scattered, buried or placed in a niche or vault in a *columbarium.* A columbarium is a building constructed for this particular purpose.

If a decision is based solely on cost, it is clear that cremation will be less expensive than burial or entombment since it will not be necessary to buy a cemetery lot or mausoleum crypt, a grave marker or monument. However, many crematoriums require that the body be placed in a casket at the time of cremation, so an inexpensive casket may be needed.

BEQUEATHAL TO A MEDICAL SCHOOL

You may desire to donate your body to medical education. All 50 states have passed the Uniform Anatomical Gift Act, which allows you to give your body to medical schools or hospitals for scientific use. Many feel that this is the least costly way of handling your remains.

Since rules and regulations differ among the various medical schools, it is necessary to familiarize yourself with the requirements of a particular medical school. Some schools require embalming; others forbid it. Some pay all costs of transportation; some pay none. Those with a surplus of bodies will accept no more; others are in desperate need of donations. Individual schools will be glad to provide you with printed materials describing their requirements and telling you how to donate your body.

The medical school will arrange for the disposition of the remains following the useful educational life of the body. This will be done at no cost to the family. If the family wishes the cremated remains returned, arrangements may be made with the medical school.

DONATION OF BODY PARTS

You may want to donate certain portions of your body for use as transplants. These donations have proved invaluable to thousands of living persons. Such organs as kidneys, hearts, lungs, skin and corneas have been successfully transplanted. In the future, many other organs may prove usable.

After the parts have been removed from the deceased, the remains can be buried, entombed or cremated exactly as though the body were intact. Most medical schools will not accept your body for anatomical study if you have made a part donation (with the exception of cornea donations). You will have to choose between a body or a part donation.

UNIFORM ANATOMICAL GIFT ACT

The Uniform Anatomical Gift Act provides a method for the individual to donate his or her body for anatomical study, or to donate body parts for transplant, by the execution of a prescribed legal document signed by the donor and two witnesses. This document has been reduced to wallet-size in the uniform donor card, which can be carried by the donor. Since speed is essential for transplantation of body parts, the donor should carry the uniform donor card so that it is readily available if he or she should die as the result of an accident. The National Institutes of Health have published a pamphlet entitled, "How to Donate the Body or Its Organs," which gives additional information and provides you with a uniform donor card. If you are interested, write to the U.S. Department of Health and Human Services, Washington, D.C., and request Publication No. (NIH) 79–776. Many States provide a uniform donor card on the backs of drivers' licenses. The front and back of two uniform donor cards appear in the forms on pages 151 and 152. They can be removed from the book and carried in your wallet.

The presence of a uniform donor card at the time of your death does not ensure that your wishes will be followed. Even though you sign a uniform donor card or other legal document, doctors are unlikely to carry out your wishes if the next of kin is opposed. Make sure your next of kin knows your wishes and is willing to abide by them.

FUNERAL SERVICES

Funeral services consist of the observances held for a deceased person before a burial or cremation. These services may include religious rites, fraternal or military procedures, a commitment service at graveside, etc. In this book, the term "funeral services" will refer to ceremonies conducted with the body of the deceased present. If the body is not present, the last observances will be called "memorial services."

A *funeral director* is a person who, as the name implies, makes all of the funeral arrangements according to the desires of the family, notifies the newspapers, makes specific arrangements with the religious leader, makes arrangements with the cemetery or crematorium and prepares the body for burial or cremation. The funeral director generally stocks an array of caskets in various price ranges so that the family may select its needs. He or she is generally familiar with the requirements of life insurance companies, unions, Social Security and the Veterans Administration so that he is able to help the family file necessary papers to obtain benefits. This individual can be invaluable to a bereaved family.

The family of a deceased may be emotionally disturbed following the death of a loved one, and may, because of guilt feelings, spend much more money for the funeral than the deceased would want. Funeral directors can provide an inexpensive service, but if the bereaved wants something more expensive, it will certainly be arranged.

You can express your wishes as to the cost of the funeral by filling out the appropriate forms at the end of this chapter. Or, you can prearrange your own funeral with the funeral director right now. Not only can you make the specific arrangements, you can also arrange for prepayment. Because of a history of abuses by a few members of the funeral industry, most of the states have established rules and conditions to protect the funeral investor from fraud. In many states the money for prepaid funeral arrangements is usually deposited in a bank account in the joint names of the arranger and the funeral director. The funeral director cannot withdraw the money until the death of the arranger. However, the arranger can always withdraw the money and terminate the arrangements. Of course, any prearrangements you make may be useless if your heirs are unaware of them.

You, or your heirs, must determine whether or not you wish your body to be *embalmed.* Embalming is the process by which blood and body fluids are removed from the corpse and a preserving fluid injected into the arteries. An embalmed body is temporarily preserved from decay. Since a decaying body could cause disease, embalming is looked upon as a health measure. It also preserves the features of the body for viewing at an open-casket funeral.

No state requires embalming if the burial or cremation occurs soon after death. If you intend to have an open casket funeral, you must, of course, opt for embalming. On the other hand, if you do not intend to let people view your body after your death, it need not be embalmed unless you so desire. Tell your heirs your wishes.

You may have specific desires as to music, or no music, at your funeral; flowers, or no flowers; certain poetry, or no poetry; military, or nonmilitary procedures; or other specific rites. Provision is made in the forms for you to express these wishes.

MEMORIAL SERVICES

Memorial services, as the term is used in this book, are similar to funeral services, except that the body of the deceased is not present. It has been buried, cremated, sent to a medical school, or perhaps even lost in a catastrophe. It may be the wishes of the deceased or the family to deal with the remains before holding formal services. Or a memorial service may be arranged because family and friends are unable to gather immediately after death. Memorial services, like funeral services, can be religious or nonreligious in character. They can be held at a church, home, funeral home, rented hall or any other place. They are in remembrance of, and with respect for, the deceased. If you prefer a memorial service to a funeral service, let your heirs know.

MEMORIAL SOCIETIES

Memorial societies have arisen throughout the country to provide members a simple, inexpensive method of handling remains. Generally, they advocate immediate cremation (without embalmment or funeral services) followed by a memorial service commemorating the deceased. Forms are provided to the members so that they may express their preferences. At the time of death, members of the society assist the family in making arrangements. Depending on the laws of the particular state, a memorial society may be able to go so far as to transfer the body from a hospital directly to a crematorium; or it may be restricted to giving only advice to the family.

MY FINAL WISHES AND GUIDE FOR SURVIVORS

General

I wish my body to be:

☐ buried in the earth.

☐ entombed in a mausoleum.

☐ cremated.

☐ bequeathed to a medical school.

☐ certain body parts donated.

☐ any of the above as determined by my heirs.

I wish that there be:

☐ a funeral service (body present).

☐ a memorial service (body not present).

☐ no service.

☐ any of the above.

I wish that a funeral, or memorial, service be held at:

☐ church.

☐ funeral home.

☐ my home.

☐ other: _____

☐ any of the above.

My preferences are as follows:

Name of church, synagogue, etc.: _____

Minister, priest, rabbi or other religious leader: _____

Funeral home: _____

☐ I am not a member of a memorial society.

☐ I am a member of a memorial society with which I have left my wishes as to the disposition of my remains. The name, address and telephone number is:

_____

_____

_____

MY FINAL WISHES AND GUIDE FOR SURVIVORS

Funeral or Memorial Service

I wish the service to be for: ☐ friends and relatives, ☐ private or ☐ other:_____

_____

I wish the casket to be: ☐ open ☐ closed

My favorite hymns/music are: _____

_____

Soloist: _____

My favorite scriptures, poems, etc., are: _____

_____

I ☐ do or ☐ do not wish flowers

Disposal of flowers: _____

☐ I am a member of the following organization (war veterans, Masons, etc.) and desire an organization service (specify name of organization): _____

I request that memorial contributions be made to: _____

I ☐ do or ☐ do not wish to be embalmed

I ☐ do or ☐ do not wish to have an interment service at graveside

I wish the expense of my funeral to be: ☐ minimal ☐ low average ☐ average

☐ high average or ☐ not limited

I prefer the following funeral home: _____

_____

I ☐ have or ☐ have not made funeral prearrangements with the funeral home

I ☐ have or ☐ have not made any prepayment of funeral expenses

If I have made any prepayment, it is a follows: _____

_____

_____

_____

_____ *(Any of the above may be continued on reverse.)*

MY FINAL WISHES AND GUIDE FOR SURVIVORS

Funeral or Memorial Service

_____

_____

_____

_____

_____

_____

_____

_____

_____

_____

_____

_____

_____

_____

_____

_____

_____

_____

_____

_____

_____

_____

_____

_____

_____

_____

MY FINAL WISHES AND GUIDE FOR SURVIVORS

Burial or Entombment

☐ I do not own, nor have legal use of, a cemetery lot or mausoleum crypt.

☐ I ☐ own or ☐ have legal use of:

☐ a cemetery lot

☐ a mausoleum crypt

The ownership of the lot or crypt is in the name of: _____

_____

The lot or crypt is located at:

Cemetery or mausoleum: _____

Address: _____

Section: _____ Lot #: _____

Other description: _____

_____

Location of deed: _____

I desire a ☐ grave marker or ☐ monument.

In addition to my name, date of birth and date of death, I would like the following to be placed thereon: _____

_____

_____

Special instructions:

_____

_____

_____

_____

_____

_____

_____

MY FINAL WISHES AND GUIDE FOR SURVIVORS

Cremation

☐ I wish my body to be cremated immediately.

☐ I wish my body to be cremated immediately and a memorial service subsequently held.

☐ I wish my body to be cremated following a funeral service.

☐ I wish my body to be cremated, but I leave the other details to my heirs.

Following my cremation, I wish my ashes:

  ☐ to be scattered (where permitted by law): _____

  _____

  ☐ to be placed in an urn and buried, or entombed: _____

  _____

  ☐ to be handled as my heirs determine

MY FINAL WISHES AND GUIDE FOR SURVIVORS

Bequeathal to a Medical School

☐ I wish my body to be bequeathed to:

Medical school: _____

Address: _____

_____

and/or

☐ any other medical school if inconvenient to send to the above, or, if not needed by the above.

I ☐ have or ☐ have not made prearrangements with the above medical school.

I realize that sometimes the above arrangements cannot be carried out. My alternative desire is for:

☐ burial or entombment

☐ cremation

and I have filled out the pertinent portion of these forms in case an alternative to body bequeathal is necessary.

☐ I have executed a uniform donor card and it is located: _____

_____

THE ABOVE BODY BEQUEST WILL NOT BE EFFECTIVE WITHOUT THE EXECUTION OF A UNIFORM DONOR CARD AND THE APPROVAL OF THE NEXT-OF-KIN.

❖❖❖❖❖

UNIFORM DONOR CARD	UNIFORM DONOR CARD

OF _____
Print or type name of Donor
In the hope that I may help others, I hereby make this anatomical gift, if medically acceptable, to take effect upon my death. The words and marks below indicate my desires.
I give: (a) _____ any needed organs or parts.
    (b) _____ only the following organs or parts:
_____
Specify the organ(s) or part(s)
for the purposes of transplantation, therapy, medical research or education.
    (c) _____ my body for anatomical study if needed.
Limitations or special wishes if any: _____
_____
	OF _____
	Print or type name of Donor
	In the hope that I may help others, I hereby make this anatomical gift, if medically acceptable, to take effect upon my death. The words and marks below indicate my desires.
	I give: (a) _____ any needed organs or parts.
	    (b) _____ only the following organs or parts:
	_____
	Specify the organ(s) or part(s)
	for the purposes of transplantation, therapy, medical research or education.
	    (c) _____ my body for anatomical study if needed.
	Limitations or special wishes if any: _____
	_____

The uniform donor cards above may be removed from the book to be carried in a wallet or purse. Both sides of a card must be completed, signed and witnessed to be valid.

MY FINAL WISHES AND GUIDE FOR SURVIVORS

Donation of Body Parts

☐ I do not wish to donate any body parts.

☐ I wish to donate any needed body parts.   *(If you are bequeathing your body to a medical school, only donate corneas from the eyes.)*

☐ I wish to donate only the following organs or parts:

　　☐ kidneys

　　☐ corneas from the eyes

　　☐ bone

　　☐ skin

　　☐ blood vessels

　　☐ cartilage

　　☐ other: _____

_____

☐ Limitations or special wishes: _____

_____

_____

☐ I have executed a uniform donor card and it is located: _____

_____

The above donations will not be effective without the execution
of a uniform donor card and the approval of the next of kin.

❖❖❖❖❖❖

Signed by the donor and the following two witnesses in the presence of each other.		Signed by the donor and the following two witnesses in the presence of each other.
_____ _____ *Signature of Donor*　　　*Date of Birth*		_____ _____ *Signature of Donor*　　　*Date of Birth*
_____ _____ *City & State*　　　*Date Signed*		_____ _____ *City & State*　　　*Date Signed*
_____ _____ *Witness*　　　*Witness*		_____ _____ *Witness*　　　*Witness*
This is a legal document under the Uniform Anatomical Gift Act or similar laws.		This is a legal document under the Uniform Anatomical Gift Act or similar laws.

The uniform donor cards above may be removed from the book to be carried in a wallet or purse.
Both sides of a card must be completed, signed and witnessed to be valid.

MY FINAL WISHES AND GUIDE FOR SURVIVORS

A Guide for My Survivors

At Time of Death: *Refer to the following forms:*

☐ Immediately authorize donation of body parts.* 152

☐ Contact medical school for body bequeathal.* 151

☐ Contact funeral director or memorial society. 146–147

☐ Notify friends, relatives and employer. 154

☐ Maintain a list of flowers, cards, donations and other expressions of sympathy.

☐ Arrange for friends and relatives to help as needed with childcare,
   shopping, cooking, telephones, etc.

☐ Arrange funeral or memorial service 147–148

☐ Arrange for cemetery lot, mausoleum or crypt.* 149

☐ Provide obituary information to newspaper. 5–7, 39–42, 59–68

☐ Arrange for after-service luncheon or gathering for friends and relatives.

☐ Obtain a minimum of eight certified copies of death certificates.

Following Funeral or Memorial Service:

☐ Send notes to acknowledge expressions of sympathy.

☐ Notify life insurance companies and file claim forms. 75–77

☐ Notify other insurance companies and file claims where applicable.
   • Medical, health, disability, accident and travel 74–80
   • Vehicle 81–82
   • Residence 78

☐ Apply for appropriate benefits:
   • Social Security benefits 90
   • Veteran's burial benefits and other applicable benefits 91
   • Pension benefits 94–95
   • Worker's Compensation benefits 93

☐ Meet with lawyer to commence probate proceedings if needed. 156
   • Take original will and copies of forms in this book. 135–138
   • Assist with inventory of assets, etc.   75–82, 90–95, 101–103, 111–114, 118–120, 122–126

☐ Notify accountant/tax preparer (unless estate lawyer is preparing final tax returns). 156
   • Take copies of appropriate forms in this book.
   • Take copies of recent tax returns.

☐ Notify stockbroker(s). 111
   • Change ownership of joint stocks by removing name of decedent. 111–114
   • Suspend any open orders of the decedent.

☐ Notify banker(s). 101–102
   • Change ownership of joint accounts by removing name of decedent. 101–103

☐ Cancel and destroy credit cards. 157

* *If applicable.*

MY FINAL WISHES AND GUIDE FOR SURVIVORS

A Guide for Survivors

The following people should be contacted in the event of my death:

Name	Address	Phone	Relationship (Friend, Employer, Cousin, etc.)

CHAPTER 10

Miscellaneous Information

When you have completed all of the preceding forms, there may be other information that you wish listed for your heirs. Only you know what that may be. Perhaps there are certain papers or letters that you wish destroyed without being opened. If so, tell your heirs about it.

You may wish to list your various credit cards and numbers with the names and addresses of the companies. These should be cancelled by your heirs after your death and the cards destroyed. (It may also be of great help if your wallet is lost or stolen.)

Maybe you have personal messages that you wish relayed to people after your death. Here is a place to do it.

In other words, these last forms are solely for your use as you see fit.

❖❖❖❖❖❖

Keep this book up to date.

Share it with your heirs.

❖❖❖❖❖❖

GOOD LUCK AND GOOD HEALTH!

MISCELLANEOUS INFORMATION

Professional Advisers

My lawyer is: _____

Address: _____

_____

My accountant/tax preparer is: _____

Address: _____

_____

Copies of my income tax returns are located: _____

_____

My dentist is: _____

Address: _____

_____

My personal physician is: _____

Address: _____

_____

My specialty physician is: _____

Address: _____

_____

My specialty physician is: _____

Address: _____

_____

My specialty physician is: _____

Address: _____

_____

My _____ is: _____
   Profession

Address: _____

_____

MISCELLANEOUS INFORMATION

Credit Cards, Etc.

I have the following credit cards:

Name of Company	Address/Telephone	Card Number

❖❖❖❖❖❖

My driver's license #: _____ Expires: _____

Passport number: _____ Date of issue: _____

Country of issue: _____ Location: _____

❖❖❖❖❖❖

Please destroy the following items without opening or reading them: _____

_____

_____

MISCELLANEOUS INFORMATION

Notes for My Heirs

_____

_____

_____

_____

_____

_____

_____

_____

_____

_____

_____

_____

_____

_____

_____

_____

_____

_____

_____

_____

_____

_____

_____

MISCELLANEOUS INFORMATION

Notes for My Heirs

MISCELLANEOUS INFORMATION

Notes for My Heirs

INDEX

DOCUMENT POCKET #1

Original documents that are valuable or irreplaceable should be kept in a safe-deposit box, and copies kept in the document pockets.

- ☐ Birth certificates
- ☐ Death certificates
- ☐ Marriage certificates
- ☐ Change of name certificates
- ☐ Divorce decrees or judgments
- ☐ Annulment decrees or judgments
- ☐ Adoption papers
- ☐ Naturalization papers
- ☐ Other _____

_____

_____

DOCUMENT POCKET #2

Original documents that are valuable or irreplaceable should be kept in a safe-deposit box, and copies kept in the document pockets.

- ☐ Educational certificates
- ☐ Educational transcripts
- ☐ Organization membership certificates
- ☐ Organization awards
- ☐ Civic awards
- ☐ Newspaper articles
- ☐ Athletic awards
- ☐ Dramatic awards
- ☐ Other _____

_____

_____